Poems of Love

ANNO
DNI
1591

ÆTATIS
SVÆ 18

JOHN DONNE

Poems of Love

Introduction by Kingsley Hart

1958

FOLIO SOCIETY

The text used for this edition is based on the Oxford
Standard Authors edition of the Poems of John Donne,
edited by Sir Herbert Grierson, by permission of the
Oxford University Press.

Fourth impression (reset) 1963

PRINTED IN GREAT BRITAIN

*Printed and bound by W. & J. Mackay & Co Ltd, Chatham
Set in 11 point Van Dijck*

Contents

EPITHALAMIONS, OR MARRIAGE SONGS

DIVINE POEMS

HOLY SONNETS

Holy Sonnets

8

Introduction

Ben Jonson told William Drummond, 'That Done himself for not being understood would perish'. For two and a half centuries after his death this prophesy was to a very large extent fulfilled. During the last fifty years or so, however, a complete revaluation has taken place; today the poetry of Donne, and in particular the love poetry, is considered by many to be among the finest in the language. The history of Donne's reputation in the intervening years before this modern revival of enthusiasm and interest consists of a series of misunderstandings and misconceptions. The concensus of two centuries of critical opinion was expressed by Hazlitt in his account of Donne and his followers: 'The complaint so often made, and here repeated, is not the want of power in these men, but the waste of it; not the absence of genius, but the abuse of it!'

Although Donne was not without his champions, he was always the connoisseur's poet. The modern reader, however, does not necessarily have to be a connoisseur of poetry in order to find that with the accumulated results of fifty years of careful scholarship and criticism to help him, he can overcome the difficulties presented by Donne's 'tortured syntax' and 'unmeaning subtlety' and approach the poetic truths which they conceal.

Izaak Walton, Donne's first biographer, gives us a clear account of Dr Donne, Dean of St Paul's, which is full of charm and sensitive appreciation. He tells us of the devout parish priest, who divided his time between private meditation and the performance of his priestly duties, and at all times revealed an intense vocational urgency. But it is Walton's portrait of Donne the preacher which provides us with a personal characteristic essential to an understanding of his poetry:

9

A Preacher in earnest, weeping, sometimes for his Auditory, sometimes with them, alwayes preaching to himselfe, like an Angel from a cloud, though in none: carrying some (as S. *Paul* was) to heaven, in holy raptures; enticing others, by a sacred art and courtship, to amend their lives; and all this with a most particular grace, and un-imitable fashion of speaking.

The histrionic skill of the preacher, his sense of drama in the preaching of God's word, his turning of the pulpit into a stage, are not irreconcilable with the portrait of the young Donne which we can reconstruct from the accounts of Walton and others. The young man about town between 1591 and 1598 is described by his contemporary at Oxford, Sir Richard Baker, as 'not dissolute, but very neat, a great visitor of Ladies, a great frequenter of Playes, a great writer of conceited Verses.' From the beginning these 'conceited Verses' reveal a sense of the dramatic, whether they are cynical and flippant outbursts on the inconstancy of women, Satires and Elegies revealing the influence of Horace and Ovid, or more serious approaches to different love relationships. Throughout, the poetic situation is dramatized:

> When I am gone, dreame me some happinesse,
> Nor let thy lookes our long hid love confesse,
> Nor praise, nor dispraise me, nor blesse nor curse
> Openly loves force, nor in bed fright thy Nurse
> With midnights startings, crying out, oh, oh,
> Nurse, ô my love is slaine, I saw him goe
> O'r the white Alpes alone; I saw him I,
> Assail'd, fight, taken, stabb'd, bleed, fall, and die.
> *Elegie* XVI: *On his Mistris*, ll.47–54

> As virtuous men passe mildly away,
>   And whisper to their soules, to goe,
> Whilst some of their sad friends doe say,
>   The breath goes now, and some say, no:
> *A Valediction: forbidding mourning*, ll.1–4

When Donne himself is at the centre of the situation, as in *Hymne to God my God, in my sicknesse*, this dramatic quality acquires an added sense of personal urgency and excitement. The same quality is present again and again in the *Sermons*, and it is tempting to suppose that after his ordination in 1615 it found its natural expression in his preaching. The connection between poet and divine becomes clearer when we realise that the same strong sense of personal drama, and the same feature of the dramatised situation are present alike in the many different approaches he makes towards earthly love and in his poetic dealings with his maker. As dramatic verse outside the context of the drama proper, Donne's is equalled only by Robert Browning.

The element of dramatic contrast is by no means lacking in the story of Donne's own life. However, the 'great visiter of Ladies' was one and the same man as the divine of whom James I could say: 'My Doctor is an honest man; And my Lords, I was never more joyed in anything that I have done, then in making him a Divine.' The rich variety to be found in his life and character provides tempting material for a modern psychological approach, and many critics have found that the various paradoxical elements between youth and age, coarse cynic and saintly divine, impatient satirist and pious preacher, cannot be reconciled. However, reconciliation is unnecessary; our final picture of the man is not of two Donnes, one coarse and cynical, the other devout and other-worldly, but of countless aspects of the same personality, all related to some point or other in the drama of his life, acquiring through his poetry a quality which we usually associate with the drama proper – that of being 'larger than life'.

Donne was born in London of Catholic parents in 1572. His mother came of a good family, numbering Mores, Rastells and Heywoods among her relations. Donne's father died when the boy was only four years old, and it is understandable that the mother should wish him to be

brought up as a Catholic. The influence of his Jesuit teachers is to be seen throughout his life, not only in his *Divine Poems* and the devotional works that occupied him as an Anglican priest, but in the authority with which he turned his hand to anti-Catholic polemic for James I and his chaplain Thomas Morton; without the thoroughness of this Catholic upbringing, Donne could not have written the *Pseudo-Martyr*.

Like the sons of other Catholic families he went to Oxford at a very early age, in order to acquire a university education before being forced to take the Oath of Supremacy at the age of sixteen. After this there is some likelihood that he was at Cambridge for three years, although this cannot be substantiated. It is also equally possible that he spent these years travelling in Italy and Spain. In 1591 he began to study law, first at Thavies Inn and later at Lincoln's Inn. Apart from the law, his studies were obviously very comprehensive and not always relevant to his ambitions. In later years Donne looked back on his student years, describing himself as:

> diverted by the worst voluptuousness, which is an Hydroptique immoderate desire of humane learning and languages: beautiful ornaments to great fortune; but mine needed an occupation, and a course.

Walton tells us that apart from his studies of a secular nature,

> he being then unresolv'd what Religion to adhere to, and considering how much it concern'd his soul to choose the most Orthodox, ... begun seriously to survey, and consider the Body of Divinity, as it was then controverted betwixt the *Reformed* and the *Roman Church*.

This was almost certainly his first concern. For a Catholic with worldly ambitions, patronage and advancement were difficult, if not impossible to obtain, and we should not suppose that Donne's decision to forsake the Catholic faith

was either a hasty or an ill-considered one; it must have entailed considerable heart-searching apart from the intense study, even if we feel that an element of practical compromise was obviously present. When Donne returned from serving under Essex in the Cadiz and Islands expeditions in 1596 and 1597, he clearly showed himself ready to conform to the requirements of the law in matters of faith, for he could not otherwise have succeeded in obtaining employment in 1598 as secretary to Sir Thomas Egerton, Keeper of the Great Seal and Lord High Chancellor. This was a good beginning towards 'some more weighty Employment in the State', and Donne was clearly labelled as a brilliant and promising young man.

During this early period, 1591–1598, Donne's verse reveals the influence not only of his studies but also of his life in London: the first four *Satires*, the *Epigrams* and most of the *Elegies* all show not only his use of the fashion of classical imitation, but also his highly individual, colloquial and racy approach to the forms he selected. However, none of these shows the same degree of originality as many of the *Songs* and *Sonets* also belonging to this period.

Walton's account of the events between the years 1598 and 1601 gives us the best impression of their significance for Donne's poetry and Donne's life. During his service with Egerton, Donne fell in love with Lady Egerton's niece, Ann More. Walton continues:

> Their love (a passion, which of all other Mankind is least able to command, and wherein most errors are committed) was in them so powerfull, that they resolved, and did marry without the approbation of those friends that might justly claime an interest in the advising and disposing of them.

It was the approbation of the young lady's father that was lacking. He was so incensed by Donne's behaviour that he did not rest until he had succeeded in persuading Egerton to dispense with the young man's services.

Donne's hope of advancement were thus ruined, and the years that followed were spent in virtual exile. Donne himself in one of the few references to his own life in his poems speaks of his 'ruin'd fortune', and doubtless poverty and the frustration of inactivity must have been at least partly responsible for the aspect of his character which became so noticeable as he grew older: a melancholic and at times almost morbid preoccupation with death, with 'the frailty and the decay of this whole world' and with the 'nothingnesse' of man. This side of his nature has often been over-emphasized; it should be remembered that 'melancholy' was characteristic of the period in general, and in poetry was associated with the best kind of 'wit'. Again, it seems unnecessary to reconcile the ambitious Donne with the melancholic; the man anxious to obtain patronage, and successful in forming friendships with the leading intellectual figures of his day, was only revealing another side of his nature when he wrote *A nocturnall upon S. Lucies day, Being the shortest day*. In later years, too, both sides are to be found in the *Sermons*.

The set-back to his fortunes resulting from his marriage was not permanent. Donne gained considerable favour at the court of James I, not only with the King himself but with a number of influential people who were anxious to help him. Among his friends and patrons at this time we find the Countess of Bedford, Mrs Herbert, Sir Robert Drury and Thomas Morton. Despite attempts to obtain secular preferment, by 1614 James had made it quite clear that he would advance Donne only in the Church. Early in 1615 he took Orders, and shortly after was appointed Reader in Divinity at Lincoln's Inn.

Apart from the prose works representing his preoccupation with religious polemic, to this period belong the finest of the *Songs and Sonets*, in particular those which refer to a relationship that must almost certainly have been his own marriage, some of the Elegies, one of the finest being *The Autumnall* written for Mrs Herbert, and the fifth *Satire*. To

the latter half of the period belong most of the *Divine Poems*, including *La Corona*, *A Litanie*, almost all the *Holy Sonnets*, and finally, *Goodfriday*, 1613. *Riding Westward*. The two *Anniversaries*, 1611–12, were written for his patron, Sir Robert Drury (whom he accompanied on missions abroad) and were the only poems to be published during Donne's lifetime.

After the death of his wife in 1617 (celebrated in the *Holy Sonnet* 'Since she whom I lov'd hath payd her last debt'), the remainder of Donne's life is the story of his wrestling with the relationship between himself and God. Although for modern readers the *Sermons*, make difficult reading, a study of them does reveal that they are intimately connected with his earlier poetry; the same qualities of 'wit', the same passionate urgency in argument are there, and they reflect the same complexity of personality. The histrionic quality reflected in the earlier *Hymne to God my God, in my sicknesse* is the same as that present in his last sermon, *Deaths Duell* preached before Charles I in Lent 1631, in the ordering of his own monument to be erected in St Paul's, and even in his instructions to his servants:

The Sunday following, he appointed his servants, that if there were any worldly businesse undone, that concerned them or himselfe, it should be prepared against Saturday next; for after that day he would not mixe his thoughts with any thing that concerned the world. Nor ever did.

Donne's relation to the poetry of his time is clearly seen in Michael Drayton's complaint in 1612 in the preface to *Poly-olbion*:

. . . in publishing this Essay of my Poeme, there is this great disadvantage against me; that it commeth out at this time, when Verses are wholly deduc't to Chambers, and nothing esteem'd in this lunatique Age, but what is kept in Cabinets, and must only passe by Transcription;

15

Donne's poetry was of this kind – written for private circulation among friends and acquaintances, and throughout it shows a man seeking an audience and taking delight in displaying the flights of his fantastic imagination, in airing his impatience with the sugary sonneteers, and in revealing the innermost secrets of his private feelings. It is understandable that apart from adopting many of the rules followed by the 'coterie' poets, he also employed many of the conventions of Drayton's kind of poetry. To both he brought a degree of originality and freshness, not to mention a strong element of parody. He rejuvenated a strain that was wearing thin by giving it a different approach in matters of language and metre, laughing at it at the same time. But more important still, he took the main ingredient of the poetry of the age – the 'conceit' – and gave it a new significance. In Donne's poetry, the conceit becomes more than an adornment to the poem; it becomes the structure upon which an argument, serious or flippant, deeply felt or merely cynically playful, is based. The 'conceit' becomes a sustained exercise of 'wit' and part of the architecture of the poem, as for example, in *The Extasie* or *The Sunne Rising*. Again and again we feel that paradox and false syllogism are not used merely as a means to impress the reader with the poet's skill and accomplishment but as the natural expression of a complex mind.

When approaching the love poetry of Donne it is essential to understand the unusual approach he makes to his subject matter. Donne made little use of the conventions of the love-lyric. His love poetry is not 'beautiful'; its music and rhythms are intricate and subtle, not simple, direct and easily grasped; he does not praise the beauty of his beloved, indeed he does not describe her physical appearance at all. Instead he tells us what it feels like – both intellectually and spiritually – to be in love. Although he is perfectly conscious of the physical side of love, he is more interested in the psychological aspect of the phenomenon. On the other hand, he is equally at home when

laughing bitterly and scornfully at the insincerity and inconstancy of so-called professions of attachment.

Dryden, who demanded much less of the poet as lover than later generations of romantically educated readers, misunderstood this approach:

> He affects the Metaphysicks, not only in his satires, but in his Amorous Verses, where Nature only should reign; and perplexes the Minds of the Fair Sex with nice Speculations of Philosophy, when he shou'd ingage their Hearts, and entertain them witn the softnesses of Love.

The proper understanding of the way in which Donne 'affects the Metaphysicks' is also of first importance. The term 'metaphysical' which has been applied to Donne and other poets of the seventeenth century is not altogether a satisfactory one, and is likely to give rise to misunderstanding. Broadly speaking, it has also come to cover the highly individual quality of intense cerebration that the verse contains, its show of scholarly learning and preoccupation with the religious and scientific problems of the day.

Saintsbury's description of this quality –

> Behind every image, every ostensible thought of his, there are vistas and backgrounds of other thoughts dimly vanishing, with glimmers in them here and there into the depths of the final enigmas of life and soul.

comes very close to the heart of the matter, but it might well be extended to apply to a vital element in the structure of the poems themselves. The first verse of *The Canonization* and the second verse of *The Anniversarie* for example, suggest that apart from the 'vistas and backgrounds of other thoughts' the verse represents the very rhythm of thought itself. The stanza division appears as a period or mental breathing space in a rapid and highly complex thought process which moves freely in the realms of metaphysics to find image and metaphor.

17

The use of the sustained conceit, the way in which he 'affects the Metaphysicks', the complex pattern provided by the rhythm of thought, and above all the histrionic element are inseparable ingredients in Donne's poetry. They have been well summarized by Mr J. B. Leishman in *The Monarch of Wit* when he characterises the poetry as 'the dialectical expression of personal drama'.

The *Songs and Sonets* can all be described as dealing with some aspect of the subject of love. They were composed over a long period, and they do not appear in chronological order; neither are they in any of the existing MSS grouped in any way that would suggest the variety they contain. The earliest are not likely to have been written earlier than 1590, and the last cannot be placed after the years immediately preceding Donne's ordination in 1615.

It is, however, possible to group them according to the attitude towards love revealed by the tone and feeling they contain. The most important are those which it is tempting to suppose were written to his wife, Ann, describing their own relationship. It is this relationship which Walton tells us was blessed 'with a mutuall, and so cordiall an affection, as in the midst of their sufferings made their bread of sorrow taste more pleasantly than the banquet of fooles'. The most important of the *Songs and Sonets* seem to speak of such a relationship, for they convey a deep sense of mutual satisfaction and fulfilment. They are: *The good-morrow, The Sunne Rising, The Canonization, Lovers infinitenesse, The Legacie, A Feaver, Aire and Angels, The Anniversarie, A Valediction: of the booke, Loves exchange, The Dreame, A Valediction: of weeping, The broken heart, A Valediction: forbidding mourning, Loves Deitie, The Dissolution, The Prohibition, The Expiration, The Computation, The Paradox, A Lecture upon the Shadow, Sonnet. The Token,* the enigmatic *A nocturnall upon S. Lucies day;* and possibly *Loves Growth* and *The Extasie.* Their most interesting characteristic is to be found in the contrast between hyperbole, 'nice Speculations of Philo-

sophy' and elaborate conceits on the one hand, and sudden
moments of simplicity and deep feeling in such lines as
these which reveal Donne's seriousness of purpose:

> And now good morrow to our waking soules,
> Which watch not one another out of feare;
>> *The good-morrow* ll.8, 9

> She'is all States, and all Princes, I,
> Nothing else is.
>> *The Sunne Rising* ll.21, 22

> Who is so safe as wee? where none can doe
> Treason to us, except one of us two.
>> *The Anniversarie* ll.25, 26

In many of the *Songs and Sonets* the attitude towards love
can, by comparison, be described as negative, 'Goe and
catche a falling starre', *Womans constancy, The Indifferent,
Loves Usury, The Triple Foole, A Valediction: of my name, in
the window, Communitie, Confined Love, Loves Alchymie, The
Flea, The Curse, Witchcraft by a picture, The Baite, The Appari-
tion, Loves diet* and *A Jeat Ring sent*, would seem to reflect
the writer of 'conceited Verses' of the earlier period. They
are often cynical or playful and sometimes coarse, but on
the whole lacking in sincerity. Their strength is often
derived from the use of the 'sustained conceit' or the tough-
ness of their colloquial language. 'Sweetest love, I do not
goe', *The Message* and *Breake of day* are quieter and more
lyrical in tone, revealing a tenderness towards the object of
Donne's thoughts reminiscent of the more conventional
approach of some of his contemporaries. *The Undertaking,
Twicknam garden, The Will, The Funerall, The Blossome, The
Primrose, The Relique* and *The Dampe*, almost certainly belong
to the middle period of Donne's life, and some of them were
inspired by Mrs Herbert and the Countess of Bedford.
They deal with definite relationships in which Donne
assumes the role of the passionate lover thrown into melancholy by the coldness of his mistress, or that of the partner

who wishes to go further than the restrictions of a platonic relationship allow.

Such a division of the *Songs and Sonets* can only be regarded as an arbitrary and generalized one, reliable only in so far as it is based on personal interpretation of the internal evidence of the poems themselves.

The resemblance between the *Songs and Sonets* and the *Divine Poems* is at many points startling. In the *Holy Sonnets* Donne's attempt to establish a relationship between himself and God reflects the moods of the lover: beseeching, despairing, impatient, ecstatic; a poem like *The Canonization* derives its great depth of feeling from an imagery and vocabulary which are distinctly religious. Sacred or prophane, human or divine, the subject can draw from Donne the same quality of intense cerebration, the same sincerity, of feeling, the same verbal attack, the same colloquial address, and above all the same histrionic skill. It was W. B. Yeats who summed up the essentially complementary nature of worldly and other-worldly elements in Donne's verse:

> The intricacies and subtleties of his imagination are the length and depth of the furrow made by his passion. His pedantry and his obscenities – the rock and the loam of his Eden – but make us the more certain that one who is but a man like us all has seen God.

K. H.

POEMS OF LOVE

The good-morrow

I wonder by my troth, what thou, and I
Did, till we lov'd? were we not wean'd till then?
But suck'd on countrey pleasures, childishly?
Or snorted we in the seaven sleepers den?
T'was so; But this, all pleasures fancies bee.
If ever any beauty I did see,
Which I desir'd, and got, t'was but a dreame of thee.

And now good morrow to our waking soules,
Which watch not one another out of feare;
For love, all love of other sights controules,
And makes one little roome, an every where.
Let sea-discoverers to new worlds have gone,
Let Maps to other, worlds on worlds have showne,
Let us possesse one world, each hath one, and is one.

My face in thine eye, thine in mine appeares,
And true plaine hearts doe in the faces rest,
Where can we finde two better hemispheares
Without sharpe North, without declining West?
What ever dyes, was not mixt equally;
If our two loves be one, or, thou and I
Love so alike, that none doe slacken, none can die.

23

Song

Goe, and catche a falling starre,
   Get with child a mandrake roote,
Tell me, where all past yeares are,
   Or who cleft the Divels foot,
Teach me to heare Mermaides singing,
Or to keep off envies stinging,
       And finde
       What winde
Serves to advance an honest minde.

If thou beest borne to strange sights,
   Things invisible to see,
Ride ten thousand daies and nights,
   Till age snow white haires on thee,
Thou, when thou retorn'st, wilt tell mee
All strange wonders that befell thee,
       And sweare
       No where
Lives a woman true, and faire.

If thou findst one, let mee know,
   Such a Pilgrimage were sweet;
Yet doe not, I would not goe,
   Though at next doore wee might meet,
Though shee were true, when you met her,
And last, till you write your letter,
       Yet shee
       Will bee
False, ere I come, to two, or three.

Womans constancy

Now thou hast lov'd me one whole day,
To morrow when thou leav'st, what wilt thou say?
Wilt thou then Antedate some new made vow?
        Or say that now
We are not just those persons, which we were?
Or, that oathes made in reverentiall feare
Of Love, and his wrath, any may forsweare?
Or, as true deaths, true maryages untie,
So lovers contracts, images of those,
Binde but till sleep, deaths image, them unloose?
        Or, your owne end to Justifie,
For having purpos'd change, and falsehood; you
Can have no way but falsehood to be true?
Vaine lunatique, against these scapes I could
        Dispute, and conquer, if I would,
        Which I abstaine to doe,
For by to morrow, I may thinke so too.

The undertaking

I have done one braver thing
  Then all the *Worthies* did,
And yet a braver thence doth spring,
  Which is, to keepe that hid.

It were but madnes now t'impart
  The skill of specular stone,
When he which can have learn'd the art
  To cut it, can finde none.

So, if I now should utter this,
  Others (because no more
Such stuffe to worke upon, there is,)
  Would love but as before.

But he who lovelinesse within
  Hath found, all outward loathes,
For he who colour loves, and skinne,
  Loves but their oldest clothes.

If, as I have, you also doe
  Vertue' attir'd in woman see,
And dare love that, and say so too,
  And forget the Hee and Shee;

And if this love, though placed so,
  From prophane men you hide,
Which will no faith on this bestow,
  Or, if they doe, deride:

Then you have done a braver thing
  Then all the *Worthies* did;
And a braver thence will spring,
  Which is, to keepe that hid.

The Sunne Rising

Busie old foole, unruly Sunne,
    Why does thou thus,
Through windowes, and through curtaines call on us?
Must to thy motions lovers seasons run?
    Sawcy pedantique wretch, goe chide
    Late schoole boyes, and sowre prentices,
  Goe tell Court-huntsmen, that the King will ride,
  Call countrey ants to harvest offices;
Love, all alike, no season knowes, nor clyme,
Nor houres, dayes, moneths, which are the rags of time.

    Thy beames, so reverend, and strong
    Why shouldst thou thinke?
I could eclipse and cloud them with a winke,
But that I would not lose her sight so long:
    If her eyes have not blinded thine,
    Looke, and to morrow late, tell mee,
  Whether both the' India's of spice and Myne
  Be where thou leftst them, or lie here with mee.
Aske for those Kings whom thou saw'st yesterday,
And thou shalt here, All here in one bed lay.

    She'is all States, and all Princes, I,
    Nothing else is.
Princes doe but play us; compar'd to this,
All honor's mimique; All wealth alchimie.
    Thou sunne art halfe as happy'as wee,
    In that the world's contracted thus;
  Thine age askes ease, and since thy duties bee
  To warme the world, that's done in warming us.
Shine here to us, and thou art every where;
This bed thy center is, these walls, thy spheare.

The Indifferent

I can love both fair and browne,
Her whom abundance melts, and her whom want betraies,
Her who loves lonenesse best, and her who maskes and
    plaies,
Her whom the country form'd, and whom the town,
Her who beleeves, and her who tries,
Her who still weepes with spungie eyes,
And her who is dry corke, and never cries;
I can love her, and her, and you and you,
I can love any, so she be not true.

Will no other vice content you?
Wil it not serve your turn to do, as did your mothers?
Or have you all old vices spent, and now would finde out
    others?
Or doth a feare, that men are true, torment you?
Oh we are not, be not you so,
Let mee, and doe you, twenty know.
Rob mee, but binde me not, and let me goe.
Must I, who came to travaile thorow you,
Grow your fixt subject, because you are true?

Venus heard me sigh this song,
And by Loves sweetest Part, Variety, she swore,
She heard not this till now; and that it should be so no
She went, examin'd, and return'd ere long,   [more.
And said, alas, Some two or three
Poore Heretiques in love there bee,
Which thinke to stablish dangerous constancie.
But I have told them, since you will be true,
You shall be true to them, who'are false to you.

Loves Usury

For every houre that thou wilt spare mee now,
                I will allow,
Usurious God of Love, twenty to thee,
When with my browne, my gray hairs equall bee;
Till then, Love, let my body raigne, and let
Mee travell, sojourne, snatch, plot, have, forget,
Resume my last yeares relict: thinke that yet
                We'had never met.

Let mee thinke any rivalls letter mine,
                And at next nine
Keepe midnights promise; mistake by the way
The maid, and tell the Lady of that delay;
Onely let mee love none, no, not the sport;
From country grasse, to comfitures of Court,
Or cities quelque choses, let report
                My minde transport.

This bargaine's good; if when I'am old, I bee
                Inflam'd by thee,
If thine owne honour, or my shame, or paine,
Thou covet most, at that age thou shalt gaine.
Doe thy will then, then subject and degree,
And fruit of love, Love I submit to thee,
Spare mee till then, I'll beare it, though she bee
                One that loves mee.

The Canonization

For Godsake hold your tongue, and let me love,
  Or chide my palsie, or my gout,
My five gray haires, or ruin'd fortune flout,
    With wealth your state, your minde with Arts improve,
        Take you a course, get you a place,
        Observe his honour, or his grace,
Or the Kings reall, or his stamped face
  Contemplate, what you will, approve,
  So you will let me love.

Alas, alas, who's injur'd by my love?
  What merchants ships have my sighs drown'd?
Who saies my teares have overflow'd his ground?
    When did my colds a forward spring remove?
        When did the heats which my veines fill
        Adde one man to the plaguie Bill?
Soldiers finde warres, and Lawyers finde out still
  Litigious men, which quarrels move,
  Though she and I do love.

Call us what you will, wee are made such by love;
  Call her one, mee another flye,
We'are Tapers too, and at our owne cost die,
    And wee in us finde the'Eagle and the Dove.
        The Phœnix ridle hath more wit
        By us, we two being one, are it.
So to one neutrall thing both sexes fit,
  Wee dye and rise the same, and prove
  Mysterious by this love.

Wee can dye by it, if not live by love,
    And if unfit for tombes and hearse
Our legend bee, it will be fit for verse;
    And if no peece of Chronicle wee prove,
        We'll build in sonnets pretty roomes;
        As well a well wrought urne becomes
The greatest ashes, as halfe-acre tombes,
    And by these hymnes, all shall approve
    Us *Canoniz'd* for Love:

And thus invoke us; You whom reverend love
    Made one anothers hermitage;
You, to whom love was peace, that now is rage;
    Who did the whole worlds soule contract, and drove
        Into the glasses of your eyes
        So made such mirrors, and such spies,
That they did all to you epitomize,
    Countries, Townes, Courts: Beg from above
    A patterne of your love!

The triple Foole

I am two fooles, I know,
For loving, and for saying so
   In whining Poëtry;
But where's that wiseman, that would not be I,
   If she would not deny?
Then as th'earths inward narrow crooked lanes
Do purge sea waters fretfull salt away,
   I thought, if I could draw my paines,
Through Rimes vexation, I should them allay,
Griefe brought to numbers cannot be so fierce,
For, he tames it, that fetters it in verse.

But when I have done so,
Some man, his art and voice to show,
   Doth Set and sing my paine,
And, by delighting many, frees againe
   Griefe, which verse did restraine.
To Love, and Griefe tribute of Verse belongs,
But not of such as pleases when'tis read,
   Both are increased by such songs;
For both their triumphs so are published,
And I, which was two fooles, do so grow three;
Who are a little wise, the best fooles bee.

Lovers infinitenesse

If yet I have not all thy love,
Deare, I shall never have it all,
I cannot breath one other sigh, to move;
Nor can intreat one other teare to fall.
And all my treasure, which should purchase thee,
Sighs, tears, and oathes, and letters I have spent,
Yet no more can be due to mee,
Then at the bargaine made was ment,
If then thy gift of love were partiall,
That some to mee, some should to others fall,
   Deare, I shall never have Thee All.

Or if then thou gavest mee all,
All was but All, which thou hadst then,
But if in thy heart, since, there be or shall,
New love created bee, by other men,
Which have their stocks intire, and can in teares,
In sighs, in oathes, and letters outbid mee,
This new love may beget new feares,
For, this love was not vowed by thee.
And yet it was, thy gift being generall,
The ground, thy heart is mine, what ever shall
   Grow there, deare, I should have it all.

Yet I would not have all yet,
Hee that hath all can have no more,
And since my love doth every day admit
New growth, thou shouldst have new rewards in store;
Thou canst not every day give me thy heart,
If thou canst give it, then thou never gavest it:
Loves riddles are, that though thy heart depart,
It stayes at home, and thou with losing savest it:
But wee will have a way more liberall,
Then changing hearts, to joyne them, so wee shall
   Be one, and one anothers All.

Song

Sweetest love, I do not goe,
    For wearinesse of thee,
Nor in hope the world can show
    A fitter Love for mee;
        But since that I
Must dye at last, 'tis best,
To use my selfe in jest
    Thus by fain'd deaths to dye;

Yesternight the Sunne went hence,
    And yet is here to day,
He hath no desire nor sense,
    Nor halfe so short a way:
        Then feare not mee,
But beleeve that I shall make
Speedier journeyes, since I take
    More wings and spurres then hee.

O how feeble is mans power,
    That if good fortune fall,
Cannot adde another houre,
    Nor a lost houre recall!
        But come bad chance,
And wee joyne to'it our strength,
And wee teach it art and length,
    It selfe o'r is to'advance.

When thou sigh'st, thou sigh'st not winde,
    But sigh'st my soule away,
When thou weep'st, unkindly kinde,
    My life blood doth decay.
        It cannot bee
That thou lov'st mee, as thou say'st,
If in thine my life thou waste,
    Thou art the best of mee.

34

Let not thy divining heart
   Forethinke me any ill,
Destiny may take thy part,
   And may thy feares fulfill;
     But thinke that wee
Are but turn'd aside to sleepe;
They who one another keepe
   Alive, ne'r parted bee.

The Legacie

When I dyed last, and, Deare, I dye
  As often as from thee I goe,
  Though it be but an houre agoe,
And Lovers houres be full eternity,
I can remember yet, that I
  Something did say, and something did bestow;
Though I be dead, which sent mee, I should be
Mine owne executor and Legacie.

I heard mee say, Tell her anon,
  That my selfe, (that is you, not I,)
  Did kill me, and when I felt mee dye,
I bid mee send my heart, when I was gone,
But I alas could there finde none,
  When I had ripp'd me, 'and search'd where hearts did lye;
It kill'd mee againe, that I who still was true,
In life, in my last Will should cozen you.

Yet I found something like a heart,
  But colours it, and corners had,
  It was not good, it was not bad,
It was intire to none, and few had part.
As good as could be made by art
  It seem'd; and therefore for our losses sad,
I mean to send this heart in stead of mine,
But oh, no man could hold it, for twas thine.

A Feaver

Oh doe not die, for I shall hate
   All women so, when thou art gone,
That thee I shall not celebrate,
   When I remember, thou wast one.

But yet thou canst not die, I know;
   To leave this world behinde, is death,
But when thou from this world wilt goe,
   The whole world vapors with thy breath.

Or if, when thou, the worlds soule, goest,
   It stay, tis but thy carkasse then,
The fairest woman, but thy ghost,
   But corrupt wormes, the worthyest men.

O wrangling schooles, that search what fire
   Shall burne this world, had none the wit
Unto this knowledge to aspire,
   That this her feaver might be it?

And yet she cannot wast by this,
   Nor long beare this torturing wrong,
For much corruption needfull is
   To fuell such a feaver long.

These burning fits but meteors bee,
   Whose matter in thee is soone spent.
Thy beauty, 'and all parts, which are thee,
   Are unchangeable firmament.

Yet t'was of my minde, seising thee,
   Though it in thee cannot persever.
For I had rather owner bee
   Of thee one houre, then all else ever.

Aire and Angels

Twice or thrice had I loved thee,
Before I knew thy face or name,
So in a voice, so in a shapelesse flame,
Angells affect us oft, and worship'd bee;
    Still when, to where thou wert, I came,
Some lovely glorious nothing I did see.
    But since my soule, whose child love is,
Takes limmes of flesh, and else could nothing doe,
    More subtile then the parent is,
Love must not be, but take a body too,
    And therefore what thou wert, and who,
        I bid Love aske, and now
That it assume thy body, I allow,
And fixe it selfe in thy lip, eye, and brow.

Whilst thus to ballast love, I thought,
And so more steddily to have gone,
With wares which would sinke admiration,
I saw, I had loves pinnace overfraught,
    Ev'ry thy haire for love to worke upon
Is much too much, some fitter must be sought;
    For, nor in nothing, nor in things
Extreme, and scatt'ring bright, can love inhere;
    Then as an Angell, face, and wings
Of aire, nor pure as it, yet pure doth weare,
    So thy love may be my loves spheare;
        Just such disparitie
As is twixt Aire and Angells puritie,
'Twixt womens love, and mens will ever bee.

Breake of day

'Tis true, 'tis day; what though it be?
O wilt thou therefore rise from me?
Why should we rise, because 'tis light?
Did we lie downe, because 'twas night?
Love which in spight of darknesse brought us hether,
Should in despight of light keepe us together.

Light hath no tongue, but is all eye;
If it could speake as well as spie,
This were the worst, that it could say,
That being well, I faine would stay,
And that I lov'd my heart and honor so,
That I would not from him, that had them, goe.

Must businesse thee from hence remove?
Oh, that's the worst disease of love,
The poore, the foule, the false, love can
Admit, but not the busied man.
He which hath businesse, and makes love, doth doe
Such wrong, as when a maryed man doth wooe.

The Anniversarie

All Kings, and all their favorites,
  All glory of honors, beauties, wits,
The Sun it selfe, which makes times, as they passe,
Is elder by a yeare, now, then it was
When thou and I first one another saw:
All other things, to their destruction draw,
  Only our love hath no decay;
This, no to morrow hath, nor yesterday,
Running it never runs from us away,
But truly keepes his first, last, everlasting day.

Two graves must hide thine and my coarse,
  If one might, death were no divorce.
Alas, as well as other Princes, wee,
(Who Prince enough in one another bee,)
Must leave at last in death, these eyes, and eares,
Oft fed with true oathes, and with sweet salt teares;
  But soules where nothing dwells but love
(All other thoughts being inmates) then shall prove
This, or a love increased there above,
When bodies to their graves, soules from their graves
    remove.

And then wee shall be thoroughly blest,
  But wee no more, then all the rest;
Here upon earth, we'are Kings, and none but wee
Can be such Kings, nor of such subjects bee;
Who is so safe as wee? where none can doe
Treason to us, except one of us two.
  True and false feares let us refraine,
Let us love nobly, and live, and adde againe
Yeares and yeares unto yeares, till we attaine
To write threescore: this is the second of our raigne.

A Valediction: of my name, in the window

I

My name engrav'd herein,
Doth contribute my firmnesse to this glasse,
   Which, ever since that charme, hath beene
   As hard, as that which grav'd it, was;
Thine eye will give it price enough, to mock
      The diamonds of either rock.

II

'Tis much that Glasse should bee
As all confessing, and through-shine as I,
   'Tis more, that it shewes thee to thee,
   And cleare reflects thee to thine eye.
But all such rules, loves magique can undoe,
      Here you see mee, and I am you.

III

As no one point, nor dash,
Which are but accessaries to this name,
   The showers and tempests can outwash,
   So shall all times finde mee the same;
You this intirenesse better may fulfill,
      Who have the patterne with you still.

IV

Or if too hard and deepe
This learning be, for a scratch'd name to teach,
   It, as a given deaths head keepe,
   Lovers mortalitie to preach,
Or thinke this ragged bony name to bee
      My ruinous Anatomie.

V

Then, as all my soules bee,
Emparadis'd in you, (in whom alone
   I understand, and grow and see,)
   The rafters of my body, bone
Being still with you, the Muscle, Sinew, and Veine,
      Which tile this house, will come againe:

VI

Till my returne, repaire
And recompact my scattered body so.
   As all the vertuous powers which are
   Fix'd in the starres, are said to flow
Into such characters, as graved bee
      When these starres have supremacie:

VII

So since this name was cut
When love and griefe their exaltation had,
   No doore 'gainst this names influence shut;
   As much more loving, as more sad,
'Twill make thee; and thou shouldst, till I returne,
      Since I die daily, daily mourne.

VIII

When thy inconsiderate hand
Flings out this casement, with my trembling name,
   To looke on one, whose wit or land,
   New battry to thy heart may frame,
Then thinke this name alive, and that thou thus
      In it offendst my Genius.

IX

And when thy melted maid,
Corrupted by thy Lover's gold, and page,
    His letter at thy pillow'hath laid,
    Disputed it, and tam'd thy rage,
And thou begin'st to thaw towards him, for this,
        May my name step in, and hide his.

X

And if this treason goe
To an overt act, and that thou write againe;
    In superscribing, this name flow
    Into thy fancy, from the pane.
So, in forgetting thou remembrest right,
        And unaware to mee shalt write.

XI

But glasse, and lines must bee,
No meanes our firme substantiall love to keepe;
    Neere death inflicts this lethargie,
    And this I murmure in my sleepe;
Impute this idle talke, to that I goe,
        For dying men talke often so.

Twicknam garden

Blasted with sighs, and surrounded with teares,
   Hither I come to seeke the spring,
   And at mine eyes, and at mine eares,
Receive such balmes, as else cure every thing;
   But O, selfe traytor, I do bring
The spider love, which transubstantiates all,
   And can convert Manna to gall,
And that this place may thoroughly be thought
   True Paradise, I have the serpent brought.

'Twere wholsomer for mee, that winter did
   Benight the glory of this place,
   And that a grave frost did forbid
These trees to laugh, and mocke mee to my face;
   But that I may not this disgrace
Indure, nor yet leave loving, Love let mee
   Some senslesse peece of this place bee;
Make me a mandrake, so I may groane here,
   Or a stone fountaine weeping out my yeare.

Hither with christall vyals, lovers come,
   And take my teares, which are loves wine,
   And try your mistresse Teares at home,
For all are false, that tast not just like mine;
   Alas, hearts do not in eyes shine,
Nor can you more judge womans thoughts by teares,
   Then by her shadow, what she weares.
O perverse sexe, where none is true but shee,
   Who's therefore true, because her truth kills mee.

A Valediction: of the booke

I'll tell thee now (deare Love) what thou shalt doe
   To anger destiny, as she doth us,
   How I shall stay, though she Esloygne me thus,
And how posterity shall know it too;
     How thine may out-endure
     Sybills glory, and obscure
     Her who from Pindar could allure,
   And her, through whose helpe *Lucan* is not lame,
And her, whose booke (they say) *Homer* did finde, and name.

Study our manuscripts, those Myriades
   Of letters, which have past twixt thee and mee,
   Thence write our Annals, and in them will bee
To all whom loves subliming fire invades,
     Rule and example found;
     There, the faith of any ground
     No schismatique will dare to wound,
   That sees, how Love this grave to us affords,
To make, to keep, to use, to be these his Records.

This Booke, as long-liv'd as the elements,
   Or as the worlds forme, this all-graved tome
   In cypher writ, or new made Idiome,
Wee for loves clergie only'are instruments:
     When this booke is made thus,
     Should againe the ravenous
     Vandals and Goths inundate us,
   Learning were safe; in this our Universe
Schooles might learne Sciences, Spheares Musick, Angels
     Verse.

Here Loves Divines, (since all Divinity
  Is love or wonder) may finde all they seeke,
  Whether abstract spirituall love they like,
Their Soules exhal'd with what they do not see,
    Or, loth so to amuze
    Faiths infirmitie, they chuse
    Something which they may see and use;
  For, though minde be the heaven, where love doth sit,
Beauty a convenient type may be to figure it.

Here more then in their bookes may Lawyers finde,
  Both by what titles Mistresses are ours,
  And how prerogative these states devours,
Transferr'd from Love himselfe, to womankinde,
    Who though from heart, and eyes,
    They exact great subsidies,
    Forsake him who on them relies,
  And for the cause, honour, or conscience give,
Chimeraes, vaine as they, or their prerogative.

Here Statesmen, (or of them, they which can reade,)
  May of their occupation finde the grounds:
  Love and their art alike it deadly wounds,
If to consider what 'tis, one proceed,
    In both they doe excell
    Who the present governe well,
    Whose weaknesse none doth, or dares tell;
  In this thy booke, such will their nothing see,
As in the Bible some can finde out Alchimy.

Thus vent thy thoughts; abroad I'll studie thee,
   As he removes farre off, that great heights takes;
   How great love is, presence best tryall makes,
But absence tryes how long this love will bee;
     To take a latitude
     Sun, or starres, are fitliest view'd
     At their brightest, but to conclude
   Of longitudes, what other way have wee,
But to marke when, and where the darke eclipses bee?

Communitie

Good wee must love, and must hate ill,
For ill is ill, and good good still,
   But there are things indifferent,
Which wee may neither hate, nor love,
But one, and then another prove,
   As wee shall finde our fancy bent.

If then at first wise Nature had
Made women either good or bad,
   Then some wee might hate, and some chuse,
But since shee did them so create,
That we may neither love, nor hate,
   Onely this rests, All, all may use.

If they were good it would be seene,
Good is as visible as greene,
   And to all eyes it selfe betrayes:
If they were bad, they could not last,
Bad doth it selfe, and others wast,
   So, they deserve nor blame, nor praise.

But they are ours as fruits are ours,
He that but tasts, he that devours,
   And he that leaves all, doth as well:
Chang'd loves are but chang'd sorts of meat,
And when hee hath the kernell eate,
   Who doth not fling away the shell?

Loves growth

I scarce beleeve my love to be so pure
     As I had thought it was,
     Because it doth endure
Vicissitude, and season, as the grasse;
Me thinkes I lyed all winter, when I swore,
My love was infinite, if spring make'it more.

But if this medicine, love, which cures all sorrow
With more, not onely bee no quintessence,
But mixt of all stuffes, paining soule, or sense,
And of the Sunne his working vigour borrow,
Love's not so pure, and abstract, as they use
To say, which have no Mistresse but their Muse,
But as all else, being elemented too,
Love sometimes would contemplate, sometimes do.

And yet no greater, but more eminent,
     Love by the spring is growne;
     As, in the firmament,
Starres by the Sunne are not inlarg'd, but showne.
Gentle love deeds, as blossomes on a bough,
From loves awakened root do bud out now.

If, as in water stir'd more circles bee
Produc'd by one, love such additions take,
Those like so many spheares, but one heaven make,
For, they are all concentrique unto thee;
And though each spring doe adde to love new heate,
As princes doe in times of action get
New taxes, and remit them not in peace,
No winter shall abate the springs encrease.

Loves exchange

Love, any devill else but you,
Would for a given Soule give something too.
At Court your fellowes every day,
Give th'art of Riming, Huntsmanship, or Play,
For them which were their owne before;
Onely I have nothing which gave more,
But am, alas, by being lowly, lower.

I aske no dispensation now
To falsifie a teare, or sigh, or vow,
I do not sue from thee to draw
A *non obstante* on natures law,
These are prerogatives, they inhere
In thee and thine; none should forsweare
Except that hee *Loves* minion were.

Give mee thy weaknesse, make mee blinde,
Both wayes, as thou and thine, in eies and minde;
Love, let me never know that this
Is love, or, that love childish is;
Let me not know that others know
That she knowes my paines, least that so
A tender shame make me mine owne new woe.

If thou give nothing, yet thou'art just,
Because I would not thy first motions trust;
Small townes which stand stiffe, till great shot
Enforce them, by warres law *condition* not.
Such in loves warfare is my case,
I may not article for grace,
Having put Love at last to shew this face.

This face, by which he could command
And change the Idolatrie of any land,
This face, which wheresoe'r it comes,
Can call vow'd men from cloisters, dead from tombes,
And melt both Poles at once, and store
Deserts with cities, and make more
Mynes in the earth, then Quarries were before.

For this, Love is enrag'd with mee,
Yet kills not. If I must example bee
To future Rebells; If th'unborne
Must learne, by my being cut up, and torne:
Kill, and dissect me, Love; for this
Torture against thine owne end is,
Rack't carcasses make ill Anatomies.

Confined Love

Some man unworthy to be possessor
Of old or new love, himselfe being false or weake,
    Thought his paine and shame would be lesser,
If on womankind he might his anger wreake,
            And thence a law did grow,
            One might but one man know;
            But are other creatures so?

Are Sunne, Moone, or Starres by law forbidden,
To smile where they list, or lend away their light?
    Are birds divorc'd, or are they chidden
If they leave their mate, or lie abroad a night?
            Beasts doe no joyntures lose
            Though they new lovers choose,
            But we are made worse then those.

Who e'r rigg'd faire ship to lie in harbors,
And not to seeke new lands, or not to deale withall?
    Or built faire houses, set trees, and arbors,
Only to lock up, or else to let them fall?
            Good is not good, unlesse
            A thousand it possesse,
            But doth wast with greedinesse.

The Dreame

Deare love, for nothing lesse then thee
Would I have broke this happy dreame,
     It was a theame
For reason, much too strong for phantasie,
Therefore thou wakd'st me wisely; yet
My Dreame thou brok'st not, but continued'st it,
Thou art so truth, that thoughts of thee suffice,
To make dreames truths; and fables histories;
Enter these armes, for since thou thoughtst it best,
Not to dreame all my dreame, let's act the rest.

As lightning, or a Tapers light,
Thine eyes, and not thy noise wak'd mee;
     Yet I thought thee
(For thou lovest truth) an Angell, at first sight,
But when I saw thou sawest my heart,
And knew'st my thoughts, beyond an Angels art,
When thou knew'st what I dreamt, when thou knew'st
Excesse of joy would wake me, and cam'st then,   [when
I must confesse, it could not chuse but bee
Prophane, to thinke thee any thing but thee.

Comming and staying show'd thee, thee,
But rising makes me doubt, that now,
     Thou art not thou.
That love is weake, where feare's as strong as hee;
'Tis not all spirit, pure, and brave,
If mixture it of *Feare, Shame, Honor,* have.
Perchance as torches which must ready bee,
Men light and put out, so thou deal'st with mee,
Thou cam'st to kindle, goest to come; Thus I
Will dreame that hope againe, but else would die.

A Valediction: of weeping

Let me powre forth
My teares before thy face, whil'st I stay here,
For thy face coines them, and thy stampe they beare,
And by this Mintage they are something worth,
    For thus they bee
    Pregnant of thee;
Fruits of much griefe they are, emblemes of more,
When a teare falls, that thou falls which it bore,
So thou and I are nothing then, when on a divers shore.

On a round ball
A workeman that hath copies by, can lay
An Europe, Afrique, and an Asia,
And quickly make that, which was nothing, *All*,
    So doth each teare,
    Which thee doth weare,
A globe, yea world by that impression grow,
Till thy teares mixt with mine doe overflow
This world, by waters sent from thee, my heaven
   dissolved so.

O more then Moone,
Draw not up seas to drowne me in thy spheare,
Weepe me not dead, in thine armes, but forbeare
To teach the sea, what it may doe too soone;
    Let not the winde
    Example finde,
To doe me more harme, then it purposeth;
Since thou and I sigh one anothers breath,
Who e'r sighes most, is cruellest, and hasts the others
   death.

Loves Alchymie

Some that have deeper digg'd loves Myne then I,
Say, where this centrique happinesse doth lie:
      I have lov'd, and got, and told,
But should I love, get, tell, till I were old,
I should not finde that hidden mysterie;
      Oh, 'tis imposture all:
And as no chymique yet th'Elixar got,
      But glorifies his pregnant pot,
      If by the way to him befall
Some odoriferous thing, or medicinall,
  So, lovers dreame a rich and long delight,
  But get a winter-seeming summers night.

Our ease, our thrift, our honor, and our day,
Shall we, for this vaine Bubles shadow pay?
      Ends love in this, that my man,
Can be as happy'as I can; If he can
Endure the short scorne of a Bridegroomes play?
      That loving wretch that sweares,
'Tis not the bodies marry, but the mindes,
      Which he in her Angelique findes,
      Would sweare as justly, that he heares,
In that dayes rude hoarse minstralsey, the spheares.
  Hope not for minde in women; at their best
  Sweetnesse and wit, they'are but *Mummy*, possest.

The Flea

Marke but this flea, and marke in this,
How little that which thou deny'st me is;
It suck'd me first, and now sucks thee,
And in this flea, our two bloods mingled bee;
Thou know'st that this cannot be said
A sinne, nor shame, nor losse of maidenhead,
   Yet this enjoyes before it wooe,
    And pamper'd swells with one blood made of two,
    And this, alas, is more then wee would doe.

Oh stay, three lives in one flea spare,
Where wee almost, yea more then maryed are,
This flea is you and I, and this
Our mariage bed, and mariage temple is;
Though parents grudge, and you, w'are met,
And cloysterd in these living walls of Jet.
   Though use make you apt to kill mee,
    Let not to that, selfe murder added bee,
    And sacrilege, three sinnes in killing three.

Cruell and sodaine, hast thou since
Purpled thy naile, in blood of innocence?
Wherein could this flea guilty bee,
Except in that drop which it suckt from thee?
Yet thou triumph'st, and saist that thou
Find'st not thy selfe, nor mee the weaker now;
   'Tis true, then learne how false, feares bee;
    Just so much honor, when thou yeeld'st to mee,
    Will wast, as this flea's death tooke life from thee.

The Curse

Who ever guesses, thinks, or dreames he knowes
Who is my mistris, wither by this curse;
    His only, and only his purse
    May some dull heart to love dispose,
And shee yeeld then to all that are his foes;
  May he be scorn'd by one, whom all else scorne,
  Forsweare to others, what to her he'hath sworne,
  With feare of missing, shame of getting, torne:

Madnesse his sorrow, gout his cramp, may hee
Make, by but thinking, who hath made him such:
    And may he feele no touch
    Of conscience, but of fame, and bee
Anguish'd, not that 'twas sinne, but that 'twas shee:
  In early and long scarcenesse may he rot,
  For land which had been his, if he had not
  Himselfe incestuously an heire begot:

May he dreame Treason, and beleeve, that hee
Meant to performe it, and confesse, and die,
    And no record tell why:
    His sonnes, which none of his may bee,
Inherite nothing but his infamie:
  Or may he so long Parasites have fed,
  That he would faine be theirs, whom he hath bred,
  And at the last be circumcis'd for bread:

The venom of all stepdames, gamsters gall,
What Tyrans, and their subjects interwish,
    What Plants, Mynes, Beasts, Foule, Fish,
    Can contribute, all ill which all
Prophets, or Poets spake; And all which shall
  Be annex'd in schedules unto this by mee,
  Fall on that man; For if it be a shee
  Nature before hand hath out-cursed mee.

The Message

Send home my long strayd eyes to mee,
Which (Oh) too long have dwelt on thee;
Yet since there they have learn'd such ill,
    Such forc'd fashions,
    And false passions,
        That they be
        Made by thee
Fit for no good sight, keep them still.

Send home my harmlesse heart againe,
Which no unworthy thought could staine;
But if it be taught by thine
    To make jestings
    Of protestings,
        And crosse both
        Word and oath,
Keepe it, for then 'tis none of mine.

Yet send me back my heart and eyes,
That I may know, and see thy lyes,
And may laugh and joy, when thou
    Art in anguish
    And dost languish
        For some one
        That will none,
Or prove as false as thou art now.

A nocturnall upon S. Lucies *day,*
Being the shortest day

'Tis the yeares midnight, and it is the dayes,
Lucies, who scarce seaven houres herself unmaskes,
    The Sunne is spent, and now his flasks
    Send forth light squibs, no constant rayes;
      The worlds whole sap is sunke:
The generall balme th'hydroptique earth hath drunk,
Whither, as to the beds-feet, life is shrunke,
Dead and enterr'd; yet all these seeme to laugh,
Compar'd with mee, who am their Epitaph.

Study me then, you who shall lovers bee
At the next world, that is, at the next Spring:
    For I am every dead thing,
    In whom love wrought new Alchimie.
      For his art did expresse
A quintessence even from nothingnesse,
From dull privations, and leane emptinesse:
He ruin'd mee, and I am re-begot
Of absence, darknesse, death; things which are not.

All others, from all things, draw all that's good,
Life, soule, forme, spirit, whence they beeing have;
    I, by loves limbecke, am the grave
    Of all, that's nothing. Oft a flood
      Have wee two wept, and so
Drownd the whole world, us two; oft did we grow
To be two Chaosses, when we did show
Care to ought else; and often absences
Withdrew our soules, and made us carcasses.

But I am by her death, (which word wrongs her)
Of the first nothing, the Elixer grown;
  Were I a man, that I were one,
   I needs must know; I should preferre
    If I were any beast,
Some ends, some means; Yea plants, yea stones detest,
And love; All, all some properties invest;
If I an ordinary nothing were,
As shadow, a light, and body must be here.

But I am None; nor will my Sunne renew.
You lovers, for whose sake, the lesser Sunne
  At this time to the Goat is runne
   To fetch new lust, and give it you,
    Enjoy your summer all;
Since shee enjoyes her long nights festivall,
Let mee prepare towards her, and let mee call
This houre her Vigill, and her Eve, since this
Both the years, and the dayes deep midnight is.

Witchcraft by a picture

I fixe mine eye on thine, and there
   Pitty my picture burning in thine eye,
My picture drown'd in a transparent teare,
    When I looke lower I espie;
      Hadst thou the wicked skill
By pictures made and mard, to kill,
How many wayes mightst thou performe thy will?

But now I have drunke thy sweet salt teares,
   And though thou poure more I'll depart;
My picture vanish'd, vanish feares,
    That I can be endamag'd by that art;
      Though thou retaine of mee
One picture more, yet that will bee,
Being in thine owne heart, from all malice free.

The Baite

Come live with mee, and bee my love,
And we will some new pleasures prove
Of golden sands, and christall brookes,
With silken lines, and silver hookes.

There will the river whispering runne
Warm'd by thy eyes, more then the Sunne.
And there the'inamor'd fish will stay,
Begging themselves they may betray.

When thou wilt swimme in that live bath,
Each fish, which every channell hath,
Will amorously to thee swimme,
Gladder to catch thee, then thou him.

If thou, to be so seene, beest loath,
By Sunne, or Moone, thou darknest both,
And if my selfe have leave to see,
I need not their light, having thee.

Let others freeze with angling reeds,
And cut their legges, with shells and weeds,
Or treacherously poore fish beset,
With strangling snare, or windowie net:

Let coarse bold hands, from slimy nest
The bedded fish in banks out-wrest,
Or curious traitors, sleavesilke flies
Bewitch poore fishes wandring eyes.

For thee, thou needst no such deceit,
For thou thy selfe art thine owne bait;
That fish, that is not catch'd thereby,
Alas, is wiser farre then I.

The Apparition

When by thy scorne, O murdresse, I am dead,
    And that thou thinkst thee free
From all solicitation from mee,
Then shall my ghost come to thy bed,
And thee, fain'd vestall, in worse armes shall see;
Then thy sicke taper will begin to winke,
And he, whose thou art then, being tyr'd before,
Will, if thou stirre, or pinch to wake him, thinke
    Thou call'st for more,
And in false sleepe will from thee shrinke,
And then poore Aspen wretch, neglected thou
Bath'd in a cold quicksilver sweat wilt lye
    A veryer ghost then I;
What I will say, I will not tell thee now,
Lest that preserve thee'; and since my love is spent,
I'had rather thou shouldst painfully repent,
Then by my threatnings rest still innocent.

The broken heart

He is starke mad, who ever sayes,
  That he hath beene in love an houre,
Yet not that love so soone decayes,
  But that it can tenne in lesse space devour;
Who will beleeve mee, if I sweare
That I have had the plague a yeare?
    Who would not laugh at mee, if I should say,
    I saw a flaske of *powder burne a day?*

Ah, what a trifle is a heart,
  If once into loves hands it come!
All other griefes allow a part
  To other griefes, and aske themselves but some;
They come to us, but us Love draws,
Hee swallows us, and never chawes:
    By him, as by chain'd shot, whole rankes doe dye,
    He is the tyran Pike, our hearts the Frye.

If'twere not so, what did become
  Of my heart, when I first saw thee?
I brought a heart into the roome,
  But from the roome, I carried none with mee:
If it had gone to thee, I know
Mine would have taught thine heart to show
    More pitty unto mee: but Love, alas,
    At one first blow did shiver it as glasse.

Yet nothing can to nothing fall,
  Nor any place be empty quite,
Therefore I thinke my breast hath all
  Those peeces still, though they be not unite;
And now as broken glasses show
A hundred lesser faces, so
    My ragges of heart can like, wish, and adore,
    But after one such love, can love no more.

A Valediction: forbidding mourning

As virtuous men passe mildly away,
   And whisper to their soules, to goe,
Whilst some of their sad friends doe say,
   The breath goes now, and some say, no:

So let us melt, and make no noise,
   No teare-floods, nor sigh-tempests move,
T'were prophanation of our joyes
   To tell the layetie our love.

Moving of th'earth brings harmes and feares,
   Men reckon what it did and meant,
But trepidation of the spheares,
   Though greater farre, is innocent.

Dull sublunary lovers love
   (Whose soule is sense) cannot admit
Absence, because it doth remove
   Those things which elemented it.

But we by a love, so much refin'd,
   That our selves know not what it is,
Inter-assured of the mind,
   Care lesse, eyes, lips, and hands to misse.

Our two soules therefore, which are one,
   Though I must goe, endure not yet
A breach, but an expansion,
   Like gold to ayery thinnesse beate.

If they be two, they are two so
   As stiffe twin compasses are two,
Thy soule the fixt foot, makes no show
   To move, but doth, if the'other doe.

And though it in the center sit,
    Yet when the other far doth rome,
It leanes, and hearkens after it,
    And growes erect, as that comes home.

Such wilt thou be to mee, who must
    Like th'other foot, obliquely runne;
Thy firmnes makes my circle just,
    And makes me end, where I begunne.

The Extasie

Where, like a pillow on a bed,
  A Pregnant banke swel'd up, to rest
The violets reclining head,
  Sat we two, one anothers best.

Our hands were firmely cimented
  With a fast balme, which thence did spring,
Our eye-beames twisted, and did thred
  Our eyes, upon one double string;

So to'entergraft our hands, as yet
  Was all the meanes to make us one,
And pictures in our eyes to get
  Was all our propagation.

As 'twixt two equal Armies, Fate
  Suspends uncertaine victorie,
Our soules, (which to advance their state,
  Were gone out,) hung 'twixt her, and mee.

And whil'st our soules negotiate there,
  Wee like sepulchrall statues lay;
All day, the same our postures were,
  And wee said nothing, all the day.

If any, so by love refin'd,
  That he soules language understood,
And by good love were growen all minde,
  Within convenient distance stood,

He (though he knew not which soule spake,
  Because both meant, both spake the same)
Might thence a new concoction take,
  And part farre purer then he came.

This Extasie doth unperplex
   (We said) and tell us what we love,
Wee see by this, it was not sexe,
   Wee see, we saw not what did move:

But as all severall soules containe
   Mixture of things, they know not what,
Love, these mixt soules doth mixe againe,
   And makes both one, each this and that.

A single violet transplant,
   The strength, the colour, and the size,
(All which before was poore, and scant,)
   Redoubles still, and multiplies.

When love, with one another so
   Interinanimates two soules,
That abler soule, which thence doth flow,
   Defects of lonelinesse controules.

Wee then, who are this new soule, know,
   Of what we are compos'd, and made,
For, th'Atomies of which we grow,
   Are soules, whom no change can invade.

But O alas, so long, so farre
   Our bodies why doe wee forbeare?
They'are ours, though they'are not wee, Wee are
   The intelligences, they the spheare.

We owe them thankes, because they thus,
   Did us, to us, at first convay,
Yeelded their forces, sense, to us,
   Nor are drosse to us, but allay.

On man heavens influence workes not so,
  But that it first imprints the ayre,
Soe soule into the soule may flow,
  Though it to body first repaire.

As our blood labours to beget
  Spirits, as like soules as it can,
Because such fingers need to knit
  That subtile knot, which makes us man:

So must pure lovers soules descend
  T'affections, and to faculties,
Which sense may reach and apprehend,
  Else a great Prince in prison lies.

To'our bodies turne wee then, that so
  Weake men on love reveal'd may looke;
Loves mysteries in soules doe grow,
  But yet the body is his booke.

And if some lover, such as wee,
  Have heard this dialogue of one,
Let him still marke us, he shall see
  Small change, when we'are to bodies gone.

Loves Deitie

I long to talke with some old lovers ghost,
  Who dyed before the god of Love was borne:
I cannot thinke that hee, who then lov'd most,
  Sunke so low, as to love one which did scorne.
But since this god produc'd a destinie,
And that vice-nature, custome, lets it be;
  I must love her, that loves not mee.

Sure, they which made him god, meant not so much,
  Nor he, in his young godhead practis'd it;
But when an even flame two hearts did touch,
  His office was indulgently to fit
Actives to passives. Correspondencie
Only his subject was; It cannot bee
  Love, till I love her, that loves mee.

But every moderne god will now extend
  His vast prerogative, as far as Jove.
To rage, to lust, to write to, to commend,
  All is the purlewe of the God of Love.
Oh were wee wak'ned by this Tyrannie
To ungod this child againe, it could not bee
  I should love her, who loves not mee.

Rebell and Atheist too, why murmure I,
  As though I felt the worst that love could doe?
Love might make me leave loving, or might trie
  A deeper plague, to make her love me too,
Which, since she loves before, I'am loth to see;
Falshood is worse then hate; and that must bee,
  If shee whom I love, should love mee.

Loves diet

To what a combersome unwieldinesse
And burdenous corpulence my love had growne,
 But that I did, to make it lesse,
 And keepe it in proportion,
Give it a diet, made it feed upon
That which love worst endures, *discretion*.

Above one sigh a day I'allow'd him not,
Of which my fortune, and my faults had part;
 And if sometimes by stealth he got
 A she sigh from my mistresse heart,
And thought to feast on that, I let him see
'Twas neither very sound, nor meant to mee.

If he wroung from mee'a teare, I brin'd it so
With scorne or shame, that him it nourish'd not;
 If he suck'd hers, I let him know
 'Twas not a teare, which hee had got,
His drinke was counterfeit, as was his meat;
For, eyeswhich rowle towards all, weepe not, but sweat.

What ever he would dictate, I writ that,
But burnt my letters; When she writ to me,
 And that that favour made him fat,
 I said, if any title bee
Convey'd by this, Ah, what doth it availe,
To be the fortieth name in an entaile?

Thus I reclaim'd my buzard love, to flye
At what, and when, and how, and where I chuse;
 Now negligent of sport I lye,
 And now as other Fawkners use,
I springe a mistresse, sweare, write, sigh and weepe:
And the game kill'd, or lost, goe talke, and sleepe.

The Will

Before I sigh my last gaspe, let me breath,
  Great love, some Legacies; Here I bequeath
  Mine eyes to *Argus*, if mine eyes can see,
  If they be blinde, then Love, I give them thee;
  My tongue to Fame; to'Embassadours mine eares;
    To women or the sea, my teares.
  Thou, Love, hast taught mee heretofore
By making mee serve her who'had twenty more,
That I should give to none, but such, as had too much
  before.

  My constancie I to the planets give;
  My truth to them, who at the Court doe live;
  Mine ingenuity and opennesse,
  To Jesuites; to Buffones my pensivenesse;
  My silence to'any, who abroad hath beene;
    My mony to a Capuchin.
  Thou Love taught'st me, by appointing mee
  To love there, where no love receiv'd can be,
Onely to give to such as have an incapacitie.

  My faith I give to Roman Catholiques;
  All my good works unto the Schismaticks
  Of Amsterdam; my best civility
  And Courtship, to an Universitie;
  My modesty I give to souldiers bare;
    My patience let gamesters share.
  Thou Love taughtst mee, by making mee
  Love her that holds my love disparity,
Onely to give to those that count my gifts indignity.

72

I give my reputation to those
Which were my friends; Mine industrie to foes;
To Schoolemen I bequeath my doubtfulnesse;
My sicknesse to Physitians, or excesse;
To Nature, all that I in Ryme have writ;
    And to my company my wit.
Thou Love, by making mee adore
Her, who begot this love in mee before,
Taughtst me to make, as though I gave, when I do but
restore.

To him for whom the passing bell next tolls,
I give my physick bookes; my writen rowles
Of Morall counsels, I to Bedlam give;
My brazen medals, unto them which live
In want of bread; To them which passe among
    All forrainers, mine English tongue.
Thou, Love, by making mee love one
Who thinkes her friendship a fit portion
For yonger lovers, dost my gifts thus disproportion.

Therefore I'll give no more; But I'll undoe
The world by dying; because love dies too.
Then all your beauties will bee no more worth
Then gold in Mines, where none doth draw it forth;
And all your graces no more use shall have
    Then a Sun dyall in a grave.
Thou Love taughtst mee, by making mee
Love her, who doth neglect both mee and thee,
To'invent, and practise this one way, to'annihilate all three.

The Funerall

Who ever comes to shroud me, do not harme
    Nor question much
That subtile wreath of haire, which crowns my arme;
The mystery, the signe you must not touch,
    For 'tis my outward Soule,
Viceroy to that, which then to heaven being gone,
    Will leave this to controule,
And keepe these limbes, her Provinces, from dissolution.

For if the sinewie thread my braine lets fall
    Through every part,
Can tye those parts, and make mee one of all;
These haires which upward grew, and strength and art
    Have from a better braine,
Can better do'it; Except she meant that I
    By this should know my pain,
As prisoners then are manacled, when they'are condemn'd
    to die.

What ere shee meant by'it, bury it with me,
    For since I am
Loves martyr, it might breed idolatrie,
If into others hands these Reliques came;
    As 'twas humility
To afford to it all that a Soule can doe,
    So,'tis some bravery,
That since you would save none of mee, I bury some of you.

The Blossome

Little think'st thou, poore flower,
  Whom I have watch'd sixe or seaven dayes,
And seene thy birth, and seene what every houre
Gave to thy growth, thee to this height to raise,
And now dost laugh and triumph on this bough,
          Little think'st thou
That it will freeze anon, and that I shall
To morrow finde thee falne, or not at all.

Little think'st thou poore heart
  That labour'st yet to nestle thee,
And think'st by hovering here to get a part
In a forbidden or forbidding tree,
And hop'st her stiffenesse by long siege to bow:
          Little think'st thou,
That thou to morrow, ere that Sunne doth wake,
Must with this Sunne, and mee a journey take.

But thou which lov'st to bee
  Subtile to plague thy selfe, wilt say,
Alas, if you must goe, what's that to mee?
Here lyes my businesse, and here I will stay:
You goe to friends, whose love and meanes present
          Various content
To your eyes, eares, and tongue, and every part.
If then your body goe, what need you a heart?

Well then, stay here; but know,
  When thou hast stayd and done thy most;
A naked thinking heart, that makes no show,
Is to a woman, but a kinde of Ghost;
How shall shee know my heart; or having none,
          Know thee for one?
Practise may make her know some other part,
But take my word, shee doth not know a Heart.

Meet mee at London, then,
    Twenty dayes hence, and thou shalt see
Mee fresher, and more fat, by being with men,
Then if I had staid still with her and thee.
For Gods sake, if you can, be you so too:
    I would give you
There, to another friend, whom wee shall finde
As glad to have my body, as my minde.

The Primrose, being at Mountgomery Castle, upon the hill, on which it is situate

Upon this Primrose hill,
Where, if Heav'n would distill
A shoure of raine, each severall drop might goe
To his owne primrose, and grow Manna so;
And where their forme, and their infinitie
Make a terrestriall Galaxie,
As the small starres doe in the skie:
I walke to finde a true Love; and I see
That 'tis not a mere woman, that is shee,
But must, or more, or lesse then woman bee.

Yet know I not, which flower
I wish; a sixe, or foure;
For should my true-Love lesse then woman bee,
She were scarce any thing; and then, should she
Be more then woman, shee would get above
All thought of sexe, and thinke to move
My heart to study her, and not to love;
Both these were monsters; Since there must reside
Falshood in woman, I could more abide,
She were by art, then Nature falsify'd.

Live Primrose then, and thrive
With thy true number five;
And women, whom this flower doth represent,
With this mysterious number be content;
Ten is the farthest number; if halfe ten
Belonge unto each woman, then
Each woman may take halfe us men;
Of if this will not serve their turne, Since all
Numbers are odde, or even, and they fall
First into this, five, women may take us all.

The Relique

When my grave is broke up againe
Some second ghest to entertaine,
(For graves have learn'd that woman-head
To be to more then one a Bed)
    And he that digs it, spies
A bracelet of bright haire about the bone,
    Will he not let'us alone,
And thinke that there a loving couple lies,
Who thought that this device might be some way
To make their soules, at the last busie day,
Meet at this grave, and make a little stay?

    If this fall in a time, or land,
    Where mis-devotion doth command,
    Then, he that digges us up, will bring
    Us, to the Bishop, and the King,
    To make us Reliques; then
Thou shalt be a Mary Magdalen, and I
    A something else thereby;
All women shall adore us, and some men;
And since at such time, miracles are sought,
I would have that age by this paper taught
What miracles wee harmelesse lovers wrought.

    First, we lov'd well and faithfully,
    Yet knew not what wee lov'd, nor why,
    Difference of sex no more wee knew,
    Then our Guardian Angells doe;
    Coming and going, wee
Perchance might kisse, but not between those meales;
    Our hands ne'r toucht the seales,
Which nature, injur'd by late law, sets free:
These miracles wee did; but now alas,
All measure, and all language, I should passe,
Should I tell what a miracle shee was.

78

The Dampe

When I am dead, and Doctors know not why,
       And my friends curiositie
Will have me cut up to survay each part,
When they shall finde your Picture in my heart,
       You thinke a sodaine dampe of love
       Will through all their sense move,
And worke on them as mee, and so preferre
Your murder, to the name of Massacre.

Poore victories! But if you dare be brave,
       And pleasure in your conquest have,
First kill th'enormous Gyant, your *Disdaine*,
And let th'enchantresse *Honor*, next be slaine,
       And like a Goth and Vandall rize,
       Deface Records, and Histories
Of your owne arts and triumphs over men,
And without such advantage kill me then.

For I could muster up as well as you
       My Gyants, and my Witches too,
Which are vast *Constancy*, and *Secretnesse*,
But these I neyther looke for, nor professe;
       Kill mee as Woman, let mee die
       As a meere man; doe you but try
Your passive valor, and you shall finde than,
Naked you'have odds enough of any man.

The Dissolution

Shee'is dead; And all which die
   To their first Elements resolve;
And wee were mutuall Elements to us,
     And made of one another.
   My body then doth hers involve,
And those things whereof I consist, hereby
In me abundant grow, and burdenous,
     And nourish not, but smother.
   My fire of Passion, sighes of ayre,
Water of teares, and earthly sad despaire,
    Which my materialls bee,
But neere worne out by loves securitie,
Shee, to my losse, doth by her death repaire,
   And I might live long wretched so
But that my fire doth with my fuell grow.
      Now as those Active Kings
   Whose foraine conquest treasure brings,
Receive more, and spend more, and soonest breake:
This (which I am amaz'd that I can speake)
    This death, hath with my store
     My use encreas'd.
And so my soule more earnestly releas'd,
Will outstrip hers; As bullets flowen before
A latter bullet may o'rtake, the pouder being more.

A Jeat Ring sent

Thou art not so black, as my heart,
  Nor halfe so brittle, as her heart, thou art;
What would'st thou say? shall both our properties by thee
    bee spoke,
  Nothing more endlesse, nothing sooner broke?

    Marriage rings are not of this stuffe;
  Oh, why should ought lesse precious, or lesse tough
Figure our loves? Except in thy name thou have bid it say,
  I'am cheap, and nought but fashion, fling me'away.

    Yet stay with mee since thou art come,
  Circle this fingers top, which did'st her thombe.
Be justly proud, and gladly safe, that thou dost dwell with
    me,
  She that, Oh, broke her faith, would soon breake thee.

Negative love

I never stoop'd so low, as they
Which on an eye, cheeke, lip, can prey,
   Seldome to them, which soare no higher
   Then vertue or the minde to'admire,
For sense, and understanding may
   Know, what gives fuell to their fire:
My love, though silly, is more brave,
For may I misse, when ere I crave,
If I know yet, what I would have.

If that be simply perfectest
Which can by no way be exprest
   But *Negatives*, my love is so.
   To All, which all love, I say no.
If any who deciphers best,
   What we know not, our selves, can know,
Let him teach mee that nothing; This
As yet my ease, and comfort is,
Though I speed not, I cannot misse.

The Prohibition

Take heed of loving mee,
At least remember, I forbade it thee;
Not that I shall repaire my'unthrifty wast
Of Breath and Blood, upon thy sighes, and teares,
By being to thee then what to me thou wast;
But, so great Joy, our life at once outweares,
Then, least thy love, by my death, frustrate bee,
If thou love mee, take heed of loving mee.

Take heed of hating mee,
Or too much triumph in the Victorie.
Not that I shall be mine owne officer,
And hate with hate againe retaliate;
But thou wilt lose the stile of conquerour,
If I, thy conquest, perish by thy hate.
Then, least my being nothing lessen thee,
If thou hate mee, take heed of hating mee.

Yet, love and hate mee too,
So, these extreames shall neithers office doe;
Love mee, that I may die the gentler way;
Hate mee, because thy love'is too great for mee;
Or let these two, themselves, not me decay;
So shall I, live, thy Stage, not triumph bee;
Lest thou thy love and hate and mee undoe,
To let mee live, O love and hate mee too.

The Expiration

So, so, breake off this last lamenting kisse,
  Which sucks two soules, and vapors Both away,
Turne thou ghost that way, and let mee turne this,
  And let our selves benight our happiest day,
We ask'd none leave to love; nor will we owe
  Any, so cheape a death, as saying, Goe;

Goe; and if that word have not quite kil'd thee,
  Ease mee with death, by bidding mee goe too.
Or, if it have, let my word worke on mee,
  And a just office on a murderer doe.
Except it be too late, to kill me so,
  Being double dead, going, and bidding, goe.

The Computation

For the first twenty yeares, since yesterday,
  I scarce beleev'd, thou could'st be gone away,
For forty more, I fed on favours past,
  And forty'on hopes, that thou would'st, they might last.
Teares drown'd one hundred, and sighes blew out two,
  A thousand, I did neither thinke, nor doe,
  Or not divide, all being one thought of you;
  Or in a thousand more, forgot that too.
Yet call not this long life; But thinke that I
Am, by being dead, Immortall; Can ghosts die?

The Paradox

No Lover saith, I love, nor any other
    Can judge a perfect Lover;
Hee thinkes that else none can, nor will agree
    That any loves but hee:
I cannot say I lov'd, for who can say
    Hee was kill'd yesterday?
Love with excesse of heat, more yong then old,
    Death kills with too much cold;
Wee dye but once, and who lov'd last did die,
    Hee that saith twice, doth lye:
For though hee seeme to move, and stirre a while,
    It doth the sense beguile.
Such life is like the light which bideth yet
    When the lights life is set,
Or like the heat, which fire in solid matter
    Leaves behinde, two houres after.
Once I lov'd and dy'd; and am now become
    Mine Epitaph and Tombe.
Here dead men speake their last, and so do I;
    Love-slaine, loe, here I lye.

Farewell to love

Whilst yet to prove,
I thought there was some Deitie in love
    So did I reverence, and gave
Worship, as Atheists at their dying houre
Call, what they cannot name, an unknowne power,
    As ignorantly did I crave:
        Thus when
Things not yet knowne are coveted by men,
    Our desires give them fashion, and so
As they waxe lesser, fall, as they sise, grow.

    But, from late faire
His highnesse sitting in a golden Chaire,
    Is not lesse cared for after three dayes
By children, then the thing which lovers so
Blindly admire, and with such worship wooe;
    Being had, enjoying it decayes:
        And thence,
What before pleas'd them all, takes but one sense,
    And that so lamely, as it leaves behinde
A kind of sorrowing dulnesse to the minde.

    Ah cannot wee,
As well as Cocks and Lyons jocund be,
    After such pleasures? Unlesse wise
Nature decreed (since each such Act, they say,
Diminisheth the length of life a day)
    This, as shee would man should despise
        The sport;
Because that other curse of being short,
    And onely for a minute made to be,
Eagers desire, to raise posterity.

        Since so, my minde
Shall not desire what no man else can finde,
    I'll no more dote and runne
To pursue things which had indammag'd me.
And when I come where moving beauties be,
    As men doe when the summers Sunne
            Growes great,
Though I admire their greatnesse, shun their heat;
    Each place can afford shadowes. If all faile,
'Tis but applying worme-seed to the Taile.

A Lecture upon the Shadow

Stand still, and I will read to thee
A Lecture, Love, in loves philosophy.
    These three houres that we have spent,
    Walking here, Two shadowes went
Along with us, which we our selves produc'd;
But, now the Sunne is just above our head,
    We doe those shadowes tread;
    And to brave clearnesse all things are reduc'd.
  So whilst our infant loves did grow,
  Disguises did, and shadowes, flow,
  From us, and our cares; but, now 'tis not so.

That love hath not attain'd the high'st degree,
Which is still diligent lest others see.

Except our loves at this noone stay,
We shall new shadowes make the other way.
    As the first were made to blinde
    Others; these which come behinde
Will worke upon our selves, and blind our eyes.
If our loves faint, and westwardly decline;
    To me thou, falsly, thine,
    And I to thee mine actions shall disguise.
  The morning shadowes weare away,
  But these grow longer all the day,
  But oh, loves day is short, if love decay.

Love is growing, or full constant light;
And his first minute, after noone, is night.

Sonnet. The Token

Send me some token, that my hope may live,
  Or that my easelesse thoughts may sleep and rest;
Send me some honey to make sweet my hive,
  That in my passion I may hope the best.
I beg noe ribbond wrought with thine owne hands,
  To knit our loves in the fantastick straine
Of new-toucht youth; nor Ring to shew the stands
  Of our affection, that as that's round and plaine,
So should our loves meet in simplicity;
  No, nor the Coralls which thy wrist infold,
Lac'd up together in congruity,
  To shew our thoughts should rest in the same hold;
No, nor thy picture, though most gracious,
  And most desir'd, because best like the best;
Nor witty Lines, which are most copious,
  Within the Writings which thou hast addrest.

Send me nor this, nor that, t'increase my store,
But swear thou thinkst I love thee, and no more.

[Selfe Love]

He that cannot chuse but love,
And strives against it still,
Never shall my fancy move;
For he loves 'gaynst his will;
Nor he which is all his own,
And can att pleasure chuse,
When I am caught he can be gone,
And when he list refuse.
Nor he that loves none but faire,
For such by all are sought;
Nor he that can for foul ones care,
For his Judgement then is nought:
Nor he that hath wit, for he
Will make me his jest or slave;
Nor a fool, for when others . . . ,
He can neither . . . . . .
Nor he that still his Mistresse payes,
For she is thrall'd therefore:
Nor he that payes not, for he sayes
Within, shee's worth no more.
Is there then no kinde of men
Whom I may freely prove?
I will vent that humour then
In mine owne selfe love.

Elegie I: Jealosie

Fond woman, which would'st have thy husband die,
And yet complain'st of his great jealousie;
If swolne with poyson, hee lay in'his last bed,
His body with a sere-barke covered,
Drawing his breath, as thick and short, as can
The nimblest crocheting Musitian,
Ready with loathsome vomiting to spue
His Soule out of one hell, into a new,
Made deafe with his poore kindreds howling cries,
Begging with few feign'd teares, great legacies,
Thou would'st not weepe, but jolly,'and frolicke bee,
As a slave, which to morrow should be free;
Yet weep'st thou, when thou seest him hungerly
Swallow his owne death, hearts-bane jealousie.
O give him many thanks, he'is courteous,
That in suspecting kindly warneth us.
Wee must not, as wee us'd, flout openly,
In scoffing ridles, his deformitie;
Nor at his boord together being satt,
With words, nor touch, scarce lookes adulterate.
Nor when he swolne, and pamper'd with great fare,
Sits downe, and snorts, cag'd in his basket chaire,
Must wee usurpe his owne bed any more,
Nor kisse and play in his house, as before.

Now I see many dangers; for that is
His realme, his castle, and his diocesse.
But if, as envious men, which would revile
Their Prince, or coyne his gold, themselves exile
Into another countrie,'and doe it there,
Wee play'in another house, what should we feare?
There we will scorne his household policies,
His seely plots, and pensionary spies,
As the inhabitants of Thames right side
Do Londons Major; or Germans, the Popes pride.

Elegie II: The Anagram

Marry, and love thy *Flavia*, for, shee
Hath all things, whereby others beautious bee,
For, though her eyes be small, her mouth is great,
Though they be Ivory, yet her teeth be jeat,
Though they be dimme, yet she is light enough,
And though her harsh haire fall, her skinne is rough;
What though her cheeks be yellow, her haire's red,
Give her thine, and she hath a maydenhead.
These things are beauties elements, where these
Meet in one, that one must, as perfect, please.
If red and white and each good quality
Be in thy wench, ne'r aske where it doth lye.
In buying things perfum'd, we aske; if there
Be muske and amber in it, but not where.
Though all her parts be not in th'usuall place,
She'hath yet an Anagram of a good face.
If we might put the letters but one way,
In the leane dearth of words, what could wee say?
When by the Gamut some Musitions make
A perfect song, others will undertake,
By the same Gamut chang'd, to equall it.
Things simply good, can never be unfit.
She's faire as any, if all be like her,
And if none bee, then she is singular.
All love is wonder; if wee justly doe
Account her wonderfull, why not lovely too?
Love built on beauty, soone as beauty, dies,
Chuse this face, chang'd by no deformities.
Women are all like Angels; the faire be
Like those which fell to worse; but such as shee,
Like to good Angels, nothing can impaire:
'Tis lesse griefe to be foule, then to'have beene faire.

For one nights revels, silke and gold we chuse,
But, in long journeyes, cloth, and leather use.
Beauty is barren oft; best husbands say,
There is best land, where there is foulest way.
Oh what a soveraigne Plaister will shee bee,
If thy past sinnes have taught thee jealousie!
Here needs no spies, nor eunuches; her commit
Safe to thy foes; yea, to a Marmosit.
When Belgiaes citties, the round countries drowne,
That durty foulenesse guards, and armes the towne:
So doth her face guard her; and so, for thee,
Which, forc'd by businesse, absent oft must bee,
Shee, whose face, like clouds, turnes the day to night,
Who, mightier then the sea, makes Moores seem white,
Who, though seaven yeares, she in the Stews had laid,
A Nunnery durst receive, and thinke a maid,
And though in childbeds labour she did lie,
Midwifes would sweare,'twere but a tympanie,
Whom, if shee accuse her selfe, I credit lesse
Then witches, which impossibles confesse,
Whom Dildoes, Bedstaves, and her Velvet Glasse
Would be as loath to touch as Joseph was:
One like none, and lik'd of none, fittest were,
For, things in fashion every man will weare.

Elegie III: Change

Although thy hand and faith, and good workes too,
Have seal'd thy love which nothing should undoe,
Yea though thou fall backe, that apostasie
Confirme thy love; yet much, much I feare thee.
Women are like the Arts, forc'd unto none,
Open to'all searchers, unpriz'd, if unknowne.
If I have caught a bird, and let him flie,
Another fouler using these meanes, as I,
May catch the same bird; and, as these things bee,
Women are made for men, not him, nor mee.
Foxes and goats; all beasts change when they please,
Shall women, more hot, wily, wild then these,
Be bound to one man, and did Nature then
Idly make them apter to'endure then men?
They'are our clogges, not their owne; if a man bee
Chain'd to a galley, yet the galley'is free;
Who hath a plow-land, casts all his seed corne there,
And yet allowes his ground more corne should beare;
Though Danuby into the sea must flow,
The sea receives the Rhene, Volga, and Po.
By nature, which gave it, this liberty
Thou lov'st, but Oh! canst thou love it and mee?
Likenesse glues love: and if that thou so doe,
To make us like and love, must I change too?
More then thy hate, I hate'it, rather let mee
Allow her change, then change as oft as shee,
And soe not teach, but force my'opinion
To love not any one, nor every one.
To live in one land, is captivitie,
To runne all countries, a wild roguery;

95

Waters stincke soone, if in one place they bide,
And in the vast sea are more putrifi'd:
But when they kisse one banke, and leaving this
Never looke backe, but the next banke doe kisse,
Then are they purest; Change'is the nursery
Of musicke, joy, life, and eternity.

Elegie IV: The Perfume

Once, and but once found in thy company,
All thy suppos'd escapes are laid on mee;
And as a thiefe at barre, is question'd there
By all the men, that have beene rob'd that yeare,
So am I, (by this traiterous meanes surpriz'd)
By thy Hydroptique father catechiz'd.
Though he had wont to search with glazed eyes,
As though he came to kill a Cockatrice,
Though he hath oft sworne, that hee would remove
Thy beauties beautie, and food of our love,
Hope of his goods, if I with thee were seene,
Yet close and secret, as our soules, we'have beene.
Though thy immortall mother which doth lye
Still buried in her bed, yet will not dye,
Takes this advantage to sleepe out day-light,
And watch thy entries, and returnes all night,
And, when she takes thy hand, and would seeme kind,
Doth search what rings, and armelets she can finde,
And kissing notes the colour of thy face,
And fearing least thou'art swolne, doth thee embrace;
To trie if thou long, doth name strange meates,
And notes thy palenesse, blushing, sighs, and sweats;
And politiquely will to thee confesse
The sinnes of her owne youths ranke lustinesse;
Yet love these Sorceries did remove, and move
Thee to gull thine owne mother for my love.
Thy little brethren, which like Faiery Sprights
Oft skipt into our chamber, those sweet nights,
And kist, and ingled on thy fathers knee,
Were brib'd next day, to tell what they did see:
The grim eight-foot-high iron-bound serving-man,
That oft names God in oathes, and onely than,

He that to barre the first gate, doth as wide
As the great Rhodian Colossus stride,
Which, if in hell no other paines there were,
Makes mee feare hell, because he must be there:
Though by thy father he were hir'd to this,
Could never witnesse any touch or kisse.
But Oh, too common ill, I brought with mee
That, which betray'd mee to my enemie:
A loud perfume, which at my entrance cryed
Even at thy fathers nose, so were wee spied.
When, like a tyran King, that in his bed
Smelt gunpowder, the pale wretch shivered.
Had it beene some bad smell, he would have thought
That his owne feet, or breath, that smell had wrought.
But as wee in our Ile emprisoned,
Where cattell onely,'and diverse dogs are bred,
The pretious Unicornes, strange monsters call,
So thought he good, strange, that had none at all.
I taught my silkes, their whistling to forbeare,
Even my opprest shoes, dumbe and speechlesse were,
Onely, thou bitter sweet, whom I had laid
Next mee, mee traiterously hast betraid,
And unsuspected hast invisibly
At once fled unto him, and staid with mee.
Base excrement of earth, which dost confound
Sense, from distinguishing the sicke from sound;
By thee the seely Amorous sucks his death
By drawing in a leprous harlots breath;
By thee, the greatest staine to mans estate
Falls on us, to be call'd effeminate;
Though you be much lov'd in the Princes hall,
There, things that seeme, exceed substantiall;
Gods, when yee fum'd on altars, were pleas'd well,
Because you'were burnt, not that they lik'd your smell;

You'are loathsome all, being taken simply alone,
Shall wee love ill things joyn'd, and hate each one?
If you were good, your good doth soone decay;
And you are rare, that takes the good away.
All my perfumes, I give most willingly
To'embalme thy fathers corse; What? will hee die?

Elegie V: His Picture

Here take my Picture; though I bid farewell,
Thine, in my heart, where my soule dwels, shall dwell.
'Tis like me now, but I dead, 'twill be more
When wee are shadowes both, then 'twas before.
When weather-beaten I come backe; my hand,
Perhaps with rude oares torne, or Sun beams tann'd,
My face and brest of hairecloth, and my head
With cares rash sodaine stormes, being o'rspread,
My body'a sack of bones, broken within,
And powders blew staines scatter'd on my skinne;
If rivall fooles taxe thee to'have lov'd a man,
So foule, and course, as, Oh, I may seeme than,
This shall say what I was: and thou shalt say,
Doe his hurts reach mee? doth my worth decay?
Or doe they reach his judging minde, that hee
Should now love lesse, what hee did love to see?
That which in him was faire and delicate,
Was but the milke, which in loves childish state
Did nurse it: who now is growne strong enough
To feed on that, which to disused tasts seemes tough.

Elegie VI

Oh, let mee not serve so, as those men serve
Whom honours smoakes at once fatten and sterve;
Poorely enrich't with great mens words or lookes;
Nor so write my name in thy loving bookes
As those Idolatrous flatterers, which still
Their Princes stiles, with many Realmes fulfill
Whence they no tribute have, and where no sway.
Such services I offer as shall pay
Themselves, I hate dead names: Oh then let mee
Favorite in Ordinary, or no favorite bee.
When my Soule was in her owne body sheath'd,
Nor yet by oathes betroth'd, nor kisses breath'd
Into my Purgatory, faithlesse thee,
Thy heart seem'd waxe, and steele thy constancie:
So carelesse flowers strow'd on the waters face,
The curled whirlepooles suck, smack, and embrace,
Yet drowne them; so, the tapers beamie eye
Amorously twinkling, beckens the giddie flie,
Yet burnes his wings; and such the devill is,
Scarce visiting them, who are intirely his.
When I behold a streame, which, from the spring,
Doth with doubtfull melodious murmuring,
Or in a speechlesse slumber, calmely ride
Her wedded channels bosome, and then chide
And bend her browes, and swell if any bough
Do but stoop downe, or kisse her upmost brow;
Yet, if her often gnawing kisses winne
The traiterous banke to gape, and let her in,
She rusheth violently, and doth divorce
Her from her native, and her long-kept course,
And rores, and braves it, and in gallant scorne,
In flattering eddies promising retorne,
She flouts the channell, who thenceforth is drie;

Then say I; that is shee, and this am I.
Yet let not thy deepe bitternesse beget
Carelesse despaire in mee, for that will whet
My minde to scorne; and Oh, love dull'd with paine
Was ne'r so wise, nor well arm'd as disdaine.
Then with new eyes I shall survay thee,'and spie
Death in thy cheekes, and darknesse in thine eye.
Though hope bred faith and love; thus taught, I shall
As nations do from Rome, from thy love fall.
My hate shall outgrow thine, and utterly
I will renounce thy dalliance: and when I
Am the Recusant, in that resolute state,
What hurts it mee to be'excommunicate?

Elegie VII

Natures lay Ideot, I taught thee to love,
And in that sophistrie, Oh, thou dost prove
Too subtile: Foole, thou didst not understand
The mystique language of the eye nor hand:
Nor couldst thou judge the difference of the aire
Of sighes, and say, this lies, this sounds despaire:
Nor by th'eyes water call a maladie
Desperately hot, or changing feaverously.
I had not taught thee then, the Alphabet
Of flowers, how they devisefully being set
And bound up, might with speechlesse secrecie
Deliver arrands mutely, and mutually.
Remember since all thy words us'd to bee
To every suitor; I, *if my friends agree;*
Since, household charmes, thy husbands name to teach,
Were all the love trickes, that thy wit could reach;
And since, an houres discourse could scarce have made
One answer in thee, and that ill arraid
In broken proverbs, and torne sentences.
Thou art not by so many duties his,
That from the worlds Common having sever'd thee,
Inlaid thee, neither to be seene, nor see,
As mine: who have with amorous delicacies
Refin'd thee'into a blis-full Paradise.
Thy graces and good words my creatures bee;
I planted knowledge and lifes tree in thee,
Which Oh, shall strangers taste? Must I alas
Frame and enamell Plate, and drinke in Glasse?
Chafe waxe for others seales? breake a colts force
And leave him then, beeing made a ready horse?

Elegie VIII: The Comparison

As the sweet sweat of Roses in a Still,
As that which from chaf'd muskats pores doth trill,
As the Almighty Balme of th'early East,
Such are the sweat drops of my Mistris breast,
And on her (brow) her skin such lustre sets,
They seeme no sweat drops, but pearle coronets.
Ranke sweaty froth thy Mistresse's brow defiles,
Like spermatique issue of ripe menstruous boiles,
Or like the skumme, which, by needs lawlesse law
Enforc'd, Sanserra's starved men did draw
From parboild shooes, and bootes, and all the rest
Which were with any soveraigne fatnes blest,
And like vile lying stones in saffrond tinne,
Or warts, or wheales, they hang upon her skinne.
Round as the world's her head, on every side,
Like to the fatall Ball which fell on Ide,
Or that whereof God had such jealousie,
As, for the ravishing thereof we die.
Thy *head* is like a rough-hewne statue of jeat,
Where marks for eyes, nose, mouth, are yet scarce set;
Like the first Chaos, or flat seeming face
Of Cynthia, when th'earths shadowes her embrace.
Like Proserpines white beauty-keeping chest,
Of Joves best fortunes urne, is her faire brest.
Thine's like worme eaten trunkes, cloth'd in seals skin,
Or grave, that's dust without, and stinke within.
And like that slender stalke, at whose end stands
The wood-bine quivering, are her armes and hands.
Like rough bark'd elmboughes, or the russet skin
Of men late scurg'd for madnes, or for sinne,
Like Sun-parch'd quarters on the citie gate,
Such is thy tann'd skins lamentable state.

And like a bunch of ragged carrets stand
The short swolne fingers of thy gouty hand.
Then like the Chymicks masculine equall fire,
Which in the Lymbecks warme wombe doth inspire
Into th'earths worthlesse durt a soule of gold,
Such cherishing heat her best lov'd part doth hold.
Thine's like the dread mouth of a fired gunne,
Or like hot liquid metalls newly runne
Into clay moulds, or like to that Ætna
Where round about the grasse is burnt away.
Are not your kisses then as filthy, and more,
As a worme sucking an invenom'd sore?
Doth not thy fearefull hand in feeling quake,
As one which gath'ring flowers, still feares a snake?
Is not your last act harsh, and violent,
As when a Plough a stony ground doth rent?
So kisse good Turtles, so devoutly nice
Are Priests in handling reverent sacrifice,
And such in searching wounds the Surgeon is
As wee, when wee embrace, or touch, or kisse.
Leave her, and I will leave comparing thus,
She, and comparisons are odious.

Elegie IX: The Autumnall

No *Spring*, nor *Summer* Beauty hath such grace,
    As I have seen in one *Autumnall* face.
Yong *Beauties* force our love, and that's a *Rape*,
    This doth but *counsaile*, yet you cannot scape.
If t'were a *shame* to love, here t'were no *shame*,
    Affection here takes *Reverences* name.
Were her first yeares the *Golden Age;* That's true,
    But now shee's *gold* oft tried, and ever new.
That was her torrid and inflaming time,
    This is her tolerable *Tropique clyme*.
Faire eyes, who askes more heate then comes from hence,
    He in a fever wishes pestilence.
Call not these wrinkles, *graves;* If *graves* they were,
    They were *Loves graves;* for else he is no where.
Yet lies not Love *dead* here, but here doth sit
    Vow'd to this trench, like an *Anachorit*.
And here, till hers, which must be his *death*, come,
    He doth not digge a *Grave*, but build a *Tombe*.
Here dwells he, though he sojourne ev'ry where,
    In *Progresse*, yet his standing house is here.
Here, where still *Evening* is; not *noone*, nor *night;*
    Where no *voluptuousnesse*, yet all *delight*.
In all her words, unto all hearers fit,
    You may at *Revels*, you at *Counsaile*, sit.
This is loves timber, youth his under-wood;
    There he, as wine in *June*, enrages blood,
Which then comes seasonabliest, when our tast
    And appetite to other things, is past.
Xerxes strange *Lydian* love, the *Platane* tree,
    Was lov'd for age, none being so large as shee,
Or else because, being yong, nature did blesse
    Her youth with ages glory, *Barrennesse*.

If we love things long sought, *Age* is a thing
    Which we are fifty yeares in compassing.
If transitory things, which soone decay,
    Age must be lovelyest at the latest day.
But name not *Winter-faces*, whose skin's slacke;
    Lanke, as an unthrifts purse; but a soules sacke;
Whose *Eyes* seeke light within, for all here's shade;
    Whose *mouthes* are holes, rather worne out, then made;
Whose every tooth to a severall place is gone,
    To vexe their soules at *Resurrection*;
Name not these living *Deaths-heads* unto mee,
    For these, not *Ancient*, but *Antique* be.
I hate extreames; yet I had rather stay
    With *Tombs*, then *Cradles*, to weare out a day.
Since such loves naturall lation is, may still
    My love descend, and journey downe the hill,
Not panting after growing beauties, so,
    I shall ebbe out with them, who home-ward goe.

Elegie X: The Dreame

Image of her whom I love, more then she,
    Whose faire impression in my faithfull heart,
Makes mee her *Medall*, and makes her love mee,
    As Kings do coynes, to which their stamps impart
The value: goe, and take my heart from hence,
    Which now is growne too great and good for me:
Honours oppresse weake spirits, and our sense
    Strong objects dull; the more, the lesse wee see.
When you are gone, and *Reason* gone with you,
    Then *Fantasie* is Queene and Soule, and all;
She can present joyes meaner then you do;
    Convenient, and more proportionall.
So, if I dreame I have you, I have you,
    For, all our joyes are but fantasticall.
And so I scape the paine, for paine is true;
    And sleepe which locks up sense, doth lock out all.
After a such fruition I shall wake,
    And, but the waking, nothing shall repent;
And shall to love more thankfull Sonnets make,
    Then if more *honour*, *teares*, and *paines* were spent.
But dearest heart, and dearer image stay;
    Alas, true joyes at best are *dreame* enough;
Though you stay here you passe too fast away:
    For even at first lifes *Taper* is a snuffe.
Fill'd with her love, may I be rather grown
Mad with much *heart*, then *ideott* with none.

Elegie XI: The Bracelet

UPON THE LOSSE OF HIS MISTRESSES CHAINE,
FOR WHICH HE MADE SATISFACTION

Not that in colour it was like thy haire,
For Armelets of that thou maist let me weare:
Nor that thy hand it oft embrac'd and kist,
For so it had that good, which oft I mist:
Nor for that silly old moralitie,
That as these linkes were knit, our love should bee:
Mourne I that I thy seavenfold chaine have lost;
Nor for the luck sake; but the bitter cost.
O, shall twelve righteous Angels, which as yet
No leaven of vile soder did admit;
Nor yet by any way have straid or gone
From the first state of their Creation;
Angels, which heaven commanded to provide
All things to me, and be my faithfull guide;
To gaine new friends, t'appease great enemies;
To comfort my soule, when I lie or rise;
Shall these twelve innocents, by thy severe
Sentence (dread judge) my sins great burden beare?
Shall they be damn'd, and in the furnace throwne,
And punisht for offences not their owne?
They save not me, they doe not ease my paines,
When in that hell they'are burnt and tyed in chains.
Were they but Crownes of France, I cared not,
For, most of these, their naturall Countreys rot
I think possesseth, they come here to us,
So pale, so lame, so leane, so ruinous;
And howsoe'r French Kings most Christian be,
Their Crownes are circumcis'd most Jewishly.

Or were they Spanish Stamps, still travelling,
That are become as Catholique as their King,
Those unlickt beare-whelps, unfil'd pistolets
That (more than Canon shot) availes or lets;
Which negligently left unrounded, looke
Like many angled figures, in the booke
Of some great Conjurer that would enforce
Nature, as these doe justice, from her course;
Which, as the soule quickens head, feet and heart,
As streames, like veines, run through th'earth's every part,
Visit all Countries, and have slily made
Gorgeous *France*, ruin'd, ragged and decay'd;
Scotland, which knew no State, proud in one day:
And mangled seventeen-headed *Belgia*.
Or were it such gold as that wherewithall
Almighty *Chymiques* from each minerall,
Having by subtle fire a soule out-pull'd;
Are dirtely and desperately gull'd:
I would not spit to quench the fire they'are in,
For, they are guilty of much hainous Sin.
But, shall my harmlesse angels perish? Shall
I lose my guard, my ease, my food, my all?
Much hope which they should nourish will be dead,
Much of my able youth, and lustyhead
Will vanish; if thou love let them alone,
For thou will love me lesse when they are gone;
And be content that some lowd squeaking Cryer
Well-pleas'd with one leane thred-bare groat, for hire,
May like a devill roare through every street;
And gall the finders conscience, if they meet.
Or let mee creepe to some dread Conjurer,
That with phantastique scheames fils full much paper;

Which hath divided heaven in tenements,
And with whores, theeves, and murderers stuft his rents,
So full, that though hee passe them all in sinne,
He leaves himselfe no roome to enter in.
But if, when all his art and time is spent,
Hee say 'twill ne'r be found; yet be content;
Receive from him that doome ungrudgingly,
Because he is the mouth of destiny.
    Thou say'st (alas) the gold doth still remaine,
Though it be chang'd, and put into a chaine;
So in the first falne angels, resteth still
Wisdome and knowledge; but, 'tis turn'd to ill:
As these should doe good works; and should provide
Necessities; but now must nurse thy pride.
And they are still bad angels; Mine are none;
For, forme gives being, and their forme is gone:
Pitty these Angels; yet their dignities
Passe Vertues, Powers, and Principalities.
    But, thou art resolute; Thy will be done!
Yet with such anguish, as her onely sonne
The Mother in the hungry grave doth lay,
Unto the fire these Martyrs I betray.
Good soules, (for you give life to every thing)
Good Angels, (for good messages you bring)
Destin'd you might have beene to such an one,
As would have lov'd and worship'd you alone:
One that would suffer hunger, nakednesse,
Yea death, ere he would make your number lesse.
But, I am guilty of your sad decay;
May your few fellowes longer with me stay
    But ô thou wretched finder whom I hate
So, that I almost pitty thy estate:
Gold being the heaviest metal amongst all,
May my most heavy curse upon thee fall:

III

Here fetter'd, manacled, and hang'd in chains,
First mayst thou bee; then chaind to hellish paines;
Or be with forraine gold brib'd to betray
Thy Countrey, and faile both of that and thy pay.
May the next thing thou stoop'st to reach, containe
Poyson, whose nimble fume rot thy moist braine;
Or libels, or some interdicted thing,
Which negligently kept, thy ruine bring.
Lust-bred diseases rot thee; and dwell with thee
Itching desire, and no abilitie.
May all the evils that gold ever wrought;
All mischiefes that all devils ever thought;
Want after plenty; poore and gouty age;
The plagues of travellers; love, marriage
Afflict thee, and at thy lives last moment,
May thy swolne sinnes themselves to thee present.
    But, I forgive; repent thee honest man:
Gold is Restorative, restore it then:
But if from it thou beest loath to depart,
Because 'tis cordiall, would twere at thy heart.

Elegie XII: His parting from her

Since she must go, and I must mourn, come Night,
Environ me with darkness, whilst I write:
Shadow that hell unto me, which alone
I am to suffer when my Love is gone.
Alas the darkest Magick cannot do it,
Thou and greate Hell to boot are shadows to it.
Should *Cinthia* quit thee, *Venus*, and each starre,
It would not forme one thought dark as mine are.
I could lend thee obscureness now, and say,
Out of my self, There should be no more Day,
Such is already my felt want of sight,
Did not the fires within me force a light.
Oh Love, that fire and darkness shoul be mixt,
Or to thy Triumphs soe strange torments fixt?
Is't because thou thy self art blind, that wee
Thy Martyrs must no more each other see?
Or tak'st thou pride to break us on the wheel,
And view old Chaos in the Pains we feel?
Or have we left undone some mutual Right,
Through holy fear, that merits thy despight?
No, no. The falt was mine, impute it to me,
Or rather to conspiring destinie,
Which (since I lov'd for forme before) decreed,
That I should suffer when I lov'd indeed:
And therefore now, sooner then I can say,
I saw the golden fruit, 'tis rapt away.
Or as I had watcht one drop in a vast stream,
And I left wealthy only in a dream.
Yet Love, thou'rt blinder then thy self in this,
To vex my Dove-like friend for my amiss:
And, where my own sad truth may expiate
Thy wrath, to make her fortune run my fate:
So blinded Justice doth, when Favorites fall,
Strike them, their house, their friends, their followers all.

Was't not enough that thou didst dart thy fires
Into our blouds, inflaming our desires,
And made'st us sigh and glow, and pant, and burn,
And then thy self into our flame did'st turn?
Was't not enough, that thou didst hazard us
To paths in love so dark, so dangerous:
And those so ambush'd round with houshold spies,
And over all, thy husbands towring eyes
That flam'd with oylie sweat of jealousie:
Yet went we not still on with Constancie?
Have we not kept our guards, like spie on spie?
Had correspondence whilst the foe stood by?
Stoln (more to sweeten them) our many blisses
Of meetings, conference, embracements, kisses?
Shadow'd with negligence our most respects?
Varied our language through all dialects,
Of becks, winks, looks, and often under-boards
Spoak dialogues with our feet far from our words?
Have we prov'd all these secrets of our Art,
Yea, thy pale inwards, and thy panting heart?
And, after all this passed Purgatory,
Must sad divorce make us the vulgar story?
First let our eyes be rivited quite through
Our turning brains, and both our lips grow to:
Let our armes clasp like Ivy, and our fear
Freese us together, that we may stick here,
Till Fortune, that would rive us, with the deed
Strain her eyes open, and it make them bleed:
For Love it cannot be, whom hitherto
I have accus'd, should such a mischief doe.
Oh Fortune, thou'rt not worth my least exclame,
And plague enough thou hast in thy own shame.
Do thy great worst, my friend and I have armes,
Though not against thy strokes, against thy harmes.
Rend us in sunder, thou canst not divide
Our bodies so, but that our souls are ty'd,

And we can love by letters still and gifts,
And thoughts and dreams, Love never wanteth shifts.
I will not look upon the quickning Sun,
But straight her beauty to my sense shall run;
The ayre shall note her soft, the fire most pure;
Water suggest her clear, and the earth sure.
Time shall not lose our passages; the Spring
How fresh our love was in the beginning;
The Summer how it ripened in the eare;
And Autumn, what our golden harvests were.
The Winter I'll not think on to spite thee,
But count it a lost season, so shall shee.
And dearest Friend, since we must part, drown night
With hope of Day, burthens well born are light.
Though cold and darkness longer hang somewhere,
Yet *Phoebus* equally lights all the Sphere.
And what he cannot in like Portions pay,
The world enjoyes in Mass, and so we may.
Be then ever your self, and let no woe
Win on your health, your youth, your beauty: so
Declare your self base fortunes Enemy,
No less by your contempt then constancy:
That I may grow enamoured on your mind,
When my own thoughts I there reflected find.
For this to th'comfort of my Dear I vow,
My Deeds shall still be what my words are now;
The Poles shall move to teach me ere I start;
And when I change my Love, I'll change my heart;
Nay, if I wax but cold in my desire,
Think, heaven hath motion lost, and the world, fire:
Much more I could, but many words have made
That, oft, suspected which men would perswade;
Take therefore all in this: I love so true,
As I will never look for less in you.

Elegie XIII: Julia

Harke newes, ô envy, thou shalt heare descry'd
My *Julia;* who as yet was ne'r envy'd.
To vomit gall in slander, swell her vaines
With calumny, that hell it selfe disdaines,
Is her continuall practice; does her best,
To teare opinion even out of the brest
Of dearest friends, and (which is worse than vilde)
Sticks jealousie in wedlock; her owne childe
Scapes not the showres of envie, To repeate
The monstrous fashions, how, were, alive, to eate
Deare reputation. Would to God she were
But halfe so loath to act vice, as to heare
My milde reproofe. Liv'd *Mantuan* now againe,
That fœmall Mastix, to limme with his penne
This she *Chymera,* that hath eyes of fire,
Burning with anger, anger feeds desire,
Tongued like the night-crow, whose ill boding cries
Give out for nothing but new injuries,
Her breath like to the juice in *Tenarus*
That blasts the springs, though ne'r so prosperous,
Her hands, I know not how, us'd more to spill
The food of others, then her selfe to fill.
But oh her minde, that *Orcus,* which includes
Legions of mischiefs, countlesse multitudes
Of formlesse curses, projects unmade up,
Abuses yet unfashion'd, thoughts corrupt,
Mishapen Cavils, palpable untroths,
Inevitable errours, self-accusing oaths:
These, like those Atoms swarming in the Sunne,
Throng in her bosome for creation.
I blush to give her halfe her due; yet say,
No poyson's halfe so bad as *Julia.*

Elegie XIV: A Tale of a Citizen and his Wife

I sing no harme good sooth to any wight,
To Lord or foole, Cuckold, begger or knight,
To peace-teaching Lawyer, Proctor, or brave
Reformed or reduced Captaine, Knave,
Officer, Jugler, or Justice of peace,
Juror or Judge; I touch no fat sowes grease,
I am no Libeller, nor will be any,
But (like a true man) say there are too many.
I feare not *ore tenus;* for my tale,
Nor Count nor Counsellour will redd or pale.
A Citizen and his wife the other day
Both riding on one horse, upon the way
I overtooke, the wench a pretty peate,
And (by her eye) well fitting for the feate.
I saw the lecherous Citizen turne backe
His head, and on his wifes lip steale a smacke,
Whence apprehending that the man was kinde,
Riding before, to kisse his wife behinde,
To get acquaintance with him I began
To sort discourse fit for so fine a man:
I ask'd the number of the Plaguy Bill,
Ask'd if the Custome Farmers held out still,
Of the Virginian plot, and whether Ward
The traffique of the I(n)land seas had marr'd,
Whether the Brittaine *Burse* did fill apace,
And likely were to give th'Exchange disgrace;
Of new-built *Algate,* and the *More-field* crosses,
Of store of Bankerouts, and poore Merchants losses
I urged him to speake; But he (as mute
As an old Courtier worne to his last suite)
Replies with onely yeas and nayes; At last
(To fit his element) my theame I cast
On Tradesmens gaines; that set his tongue agoing:
Alas, good sir (quoth he) *There is no doing*

In Court nor City now; she smil'd and I,
And (in my conscience) both gave him the lie
In one met thought: but he went on apace,
And at the present time with such a face
He rail'd, as fray'd me; for he gave no praise,
To any but my Lord of *Essex* dayes;
Call'd those the age of action; true (quoth Hee)
There's now as great an itch of bravery,
And heat of taking up, but cold lay downe,
For, put to push of pay, away they runne;
Our onely City trades of hope now are
Bawd, Tavern-keeper, Whore and Scrivener;
The much of Privileg'd kingsmen, and the store
Of fresh protections make the rest all poore;
In the first state of their Creation,
Though many stoutly stand, yet proves not one
A righteous pay-master. Thus ranne he on
In a continued rage: so void of reason
Seem'd his harsh talke, I sweat for feare of treason.
And (troth) how could I lesse? when in the prayer
For the protection of the wise Lord Major,
And his wise brethrens worships, when one prayeth,
He swore that none could say Amen with faith.
To get him off from what I glowed to heare,
(In happy time) an Angel did appeare,
The bright Signe of a lov'd and wel-try'd Inne,
Where many Citizens with their wives have bin
Well us'd and often; here I pray'd him stay,
To take some due refreshment by the way.
Looke how hee look'd that hid the gold (his hope)
And at's returne found nothing but a Rope,
So he on me, refus'd and made away,
Though willing she pleaded a weary day:
I found my misse, struck hands, and praid him tell
(To hold acquaintance still) where he did dwell;
He barely nam'd the street, promis'd the Wine,
But his kinde wife gave me the very Signe.

Elegie XV: The Expostulation

To make the doubt cleare, that no woman's true,
  Was it my fate to prove it strong in you?
Thought I, but one had breathed purest aire,
  And must she needs be false because she's faire?
Is it your beauties marke, or of your youth,
  Or your perfection, not to study truth?
Or thinke you heaven is deafe, or hath no eyes?
  Or those it hath, smile at your perjuries?
Are vowes so cheape with women, or the matter
  Whereof they are made, that they are writ in water,
And blowne away with winde? Or doth their breath
  (Both hot and cold at once) make life and death?
Who could have thought so many accents sweet
  Form'd into words, so many sighs should meete
As from our hearts, so many oathes, and teares
  Sprinkled among, (all sweeter by our feares
And the divine impression of stolne kisses,
  That seal'd the rest) should now prove empty blisses?
Did you draw bonds to forfet? signe to breake?
  Or must we reade you quite from what you speake,
And finde the truth out the wrong way? or must
  Hee first desire you false, would wish you just?
O I prophane, though most of women be
  This kinde of beast, my thought shall except thee;
My dearest love, though froward jealousie,
  With circumstance might urge thy'inconstancie,
Sooner I'll thinke the Sunne will cease to cheare
  The teeming earth, and *that* forget to beare,
Sooner that rivers will runne back, or Thames
  With ribs of Ice in June would bind his streames,
Or Nature, by whose strength the world endures,
  Would change her course, before you alter yours.
But O that treacherous breast to whom weake you
  Did trust our Counsells, and wee both may rue,

Having his falshood found too late, 'twas hee
    That made me *cast* you guilty, and you me,
Whilst he, black wretch, betray'd each simple word
    Wee spake, unto the cunning of a third.
Curst may hee be, that so our love hath slaine,
    And wander on the earth, wretched as *Cain*,
Wretched as hee, and not deserve least pitty;
    In plaguing him, let misery be witty;
Let all eyes shunne him, and hee shunne each eye,
    Till hee be noysome as his infamie;
May he without remorse deny God thrice,
    And not be trusted more on his Soules price;
And after all selfe torment, when hee dyes,
    May Wolves teare out his heart, Vultures his eyes,
Swine eate his bowels, and his falser tongue
    That utter'd all, be to some Raven flung,
And let his carrion coarse be a longer feast
    To the Kings dogges, then any other beast.
Now have I curst, let us our love revive;
    In mee the flame was never more alive;
I could beginne againe to court and praise,
    And in that pleasure lengthen the short dayes
Of my lifes lease; like Painters that do take
    Delight, not in made worke, but whiles they make;
I could renew those times, when first I saw
    Love in your eyes, that gave my tongue the law
To like what you lik'd; and at maskes and playes
    Commend the self same Actors, the same wayes;
Aske how you did, and often with intent
    Of being officious, be impertinent;
All which were such soft pastimes, as in these
    Love was as subtilly catch'd, as a disease;
But being got it is a treasure sweet,
    Which to defend is harder then to get:
And ought not be prophan'd on either part,
    For though 'tis got by *chance*, 'tis kept by *art*.

Elegie XVI: On his Mistris

By our first strange and fatall interview,
By all desires which thereof did ensue,
By our long starving hopes, by that remorse
Which my words masculine perswasive force
Begot in thee, and by the memory
Of hurts, which spies and rivals threatned me,
I calmly beg: But by thy fathers wrath,
By all paines, which want and divorcement hath,
I conjure thee, and all the oathes which I
And thou have sworne to seale joynt constancy,
Here I unsweare, and overswear them thus,
Thou shalt not love by wayes so dangerous.
Temper, ô faire Love, loves impetuous rage,
Be my true Mistris still, not my faign'd Page;
I'll goe, and, by thy kinde leave, leave behinde
Thee, onely worthy to nurse in my minde,
Thirst to come backe; ô if thou die before,
My soule from other lands to thee shall soare.
Thy (else Almighty) beautie cannot move
Rage from the Seas, nor thy love teach them love,
Nor tame wilde Boreas harshnesse; Thou hast reade
How roughly hee in peeces shivered
Faire Orithea, whom he swore he lov'd.
Fall ill or good, 'tis madnesse to have prov'd
Dangers unurg'd; Feed on this flattery,
That absent Lovers one in th'other be.
Dissemble nothing, not a boy, nor change
Thy bodies habite, nor mindes; bee not strange
To thy selfe onely; All will spie in thy face
A blushing womanly discovering grace;
Richly cloath'd Apes, are call'd Apes, and as soone
Ecclips'd as bright we call the Moone the Moone.

Men of France, changeable Camelions,
Spittles of diseases, shops of fashions,
Loves fuellers, and the rightest company
Of Players, which upon the worlds stage be,
Will quickly know thee, and no lesse, alas!
The'indifferent Italian, as we passe
His warme land, well content to thinke thee Page,
Will hunt thee with such lust, and hideous rage,
As *Lots* faire guests were vext. But none of these
Nor spungy hydroptique Dutch shall thee displease,
If thou stay here. O stay here, for, for thee
England is onely a worthy Gallerie,
To walke in expectation, till from thence
Our greatest King call thee to his presence.
When I am gone, dreame me some happinesse,
Nor let thy lookes our long hid love confesse,
Nor praise, nor dispraise me, nor blesse nor curse
Openly loves force, nor in bed fright thy Nurse
With midnights startings, crying out, oh, oh
Nurse, ô my love is slaine, I saw him goe
O'r the white Alpes alone; I saw him I,
Assail'd, fight, taken, stabb'd, bleed, fall, and die.
Augure me better chance, except dread *Jove*
Thinke it enough for me to'have had thy love.

Elegie XVII: [Variety]

The heavens rejoyce in motion, why should I
Abjure me so much lov'd variety,
And not with many youth and love divide?
Pleasure is none, if not diversifi'd:
The sun that sitting in the chaire of light
Sheds flame into what else so ever doth seem bright,
Is not contented at one Signe to Inne,
But ends his year and with a new beginnes.
All things doe willingly in change delight,
The fruitfull mother of our appetite:
Rivers the clearer and more pleasing are,
Where their fair spreading streames run wide and farr;
And a dead lake that no strange bark doth greet,
Corrupts it self and what doth live in it.
Let no man tell me such a one is faire,
And worthy all alone my love to share.
Nature in her hath done the liberall part
Of a kinde Mistresse, and imploy'd her art
To make her loveable, and I aver
Him not humane that would turn back from her:
I love her well, and would, if need were, dye
To doe her service. But followes it that I
Must serve her onely, when I may have choice
Of other beauties, and in change rejoice?
The law is hard, and shall not have my voice.
The last I saw in all extreames is faire,
And holds me in the Sun-beames of her haire;
Her nymph-like features such agreements have
That I could venture with her to the grave:
Another's brown, I like her not the worse,
Her tongue is soft and takes me with discourse.

Others, for that they well descended are,
Do in my love obtain as large a share;
And though they be not fair, 'tis much with mee
To win their love onely for their degree.
And though I faile of my required ends,
The attempt is glorious and it self commends.
How happy were our Syres in ancient times,
Who held plurality of loves no crime!
With them it was accounted charity
To stirre up race of all indifferently;
Kindreds were not exempted from the bands:
Which with the Persian still in usage stands.
Women were then no sooner asked then won,
And what they did was honest and well done.
But since this title honour hath been us'd,
Our weake credulity hath been abus'd;
The golden laws of nature are repeald,
Which our first Fathers in such reverence held;
Our liberty's revers'd, our Charter's gone,
And we're made servants to opinion,
A monster in no certain shape attir'd,
And whose original is much desir'd,
Formelesse at first, but growing on it fashions,
And doth prescribe manners and laws to nations.
Here love reciv'd immedicable harmes,
And was dispoiled of his daring armes.
A greater want then is his daring eyes,
He lost those awfull wings with which he flies;
His sinewy bow, and those immortall darts
Wherewith he'is wont to bruise resisting hearts.
Onely some few strong in themselves and free
Retain the seeds of antient liberty,
Following that part of Love although deprest,
And make a throne for him within their brest,

In spight of modern censures him avowing
Their Soveraigne, all service him allowing.
Amongst which troop although I am the least,
Yet equall in perfection with the best,
I glory in subjection of his hand,
Nor ever did decline his least command:
For in whatever forme the message came
My heart did open and receive the same.
But time will in his course a point discry
When I this loved service must deny,
For our allegiance temporary is,
With firmer age returnes our liberties.
What time in years and judgement we repos'd,
Shall not so easily be to change dispos'd,
Nor to the art of severall eyes obeying;
But beauty with true worth securely weighing,
Which being found assembled in some one,
Wee'l love her ever, and love her alone.

Elegie XVIII: *Loves Progress*

Who ever loves, if he do not propose
The right true end of love, he's one that goes
To sea for nothing but to make him sick:
Love is a bear-whelp born, if we o're lick
Our love, and force it new strange shapes to take,
We erre, and of a lump a monster make.
Were not a Calf a monster that were grown
Fac'd like a man, though better then his own?
Perfection is in unitie: preferr
One woman, first, and then one thing in her.
I, when I value gold, may think upon
The ductilness, the application,
The wholsomness, the ingenuitie,
From rust, from soil, from fire ever free:
But if I love it, 'tis because 'tis made
By our new nature (Use) the soul of trade.
    All these in women we might think upon
(If women had them) and yet love but one.
Can men more injure women then to say
They love them for that, by which they're not they?
Makes virtue woman? must I cool my bloud
Till I both be, and find one wise and good?
May barren Angels love so. But if we
Make love to woman; virtue is not she:
As beauty'is not nor wealth: He that strayes thus
From her to hers, is more adulterous,
Then if he took her maid. Search every spheare
And firmament, our *Cupid* is not there:
He's an infernal god and under ground,
With *Pluto* dwells, where gold and fire abound:
Men to such Gods, their sacrificing Coles
Did not in Altars lay, but pits and holes.

Although we see Celestial bodies move
Above the earth, the earth we Till and love:
So we her ayres contemplate, words and heart,
And virtues; but we love the Centrique part.

   Nor is the soul more worthy, or more fit
For love, then this, as infinite as it.
But in attaining this desired place
How much they erre; that set out at the face?
The hair a Forest is of Ambushes,
Of springes, snares, fetters and manacles:
The brow becalms us when 'tis smooth and plain,
And when 'tis wrinckled, shipwracks us again.
Smooth, 'tis a Paradice, where we would have
Immortal stay, and wrinkled 'tis our grave.
The Nose (like to the first Meridian) runs
Not 'twixt an East and West, but 'twixt two suns;
It leaves a Cheek, a rosie Hemisphere
On either side, and then directs us where
Upon the Islands fortunate we fall,
(Not faynte *Canaries*, but *Ambrosiall*)
Her swelling lips; To which when wee are come,
We anchor there, and think our selves at home,
For they seem all: there Syrens songs, and there
Wise Delphick Oracles do fill the ear;
There in a Creek where chosen pearls do swell,
The Remora, her cleaving tongue doth dwell.
These, and the glorious Promontory, her Chin
Ore past; and the streight *Hellespont* betweene
The *Sestos* and *Abydos* of her breasts,
(Not of two Lovers, but two Loves the neasts)
Succeeds a boundless sea, but yet thine eye
Some Island moles may scattered there descry;
And Sailing towards her *India*, in that way
Shall at her fair Atlantick Navell stay;

Though thence the Current be thy Pilot made,
Yet ere thou be where thou wouldst be embay'd,
Thou shalt upon another Forest set,
Where many Shipwrack, and no further get.
When thou art there, consider what this chace
Mispent by thy beginning at the face.
   Rather set out below; practice my Art,
Some Symetry the foot hath with that part
Which thou dost seek, and is thy Map for that
Lovely enough to stop, but not stay at:
Least subject to disguise and change it is;
Men say the Devil never can change his.
It is the Emblem that hath figured
Firmness; 'tis the first part that comes to bed.
Civilitie we see refin'd: the kiss
Which at the face began, transplanted is,
Since to the hand, since to the Imperial knee,
Now at the Papal foot delights to be:
If Kings think that the nearer way, and do
Rise from the foot, Lovers may do so too;
For as free Spheres move faster far then can
Birds, whom the air resists, so may that man
Which goes this empty and Ætherial way,
Then if at Beauties elements he stay.
Rich Nature hath in women wisely made
Two purses, and their mouths aversely laid:
They then, which to the lower tribute owe,
That way which that Exchequer looks, must go:
He which doth not, his error is as great,
As who by Clyster gave the Stomack meat.

Elegie XIX: Going to Bed

Come, Madam, come, all rest my powers defile,
Until I labour, I in labour lie.
The foe oft-times having the foe in sight,
Is tir'd with standing though he never fight.
Off with that girdle, like heavens Zone glittering,
But a far fairer world incompassing.
Unpin that spangled breastplate which you wear,
That th'eyes of busie fooles may be stopt there.
Unlace your self, for that harmonious chyme,
Tells me from you, that now it is bed time.
Off with that happy busk, which I envie,
That still can be, and still can stand so nigh.
Your gown going off, such beautious state reveals,
As when from flowry meads th'hills shadow steales.
Off with that wyerie Coronet and shew
The haiery Diademe which on you doth grow:
Now off with those shooes, and then safely tread
In this loves hallow'd temple, this soft bed.
In such white robes, heaven's Angels us'd to be
Receavd by men; Thou Angel bringst with thee
A heaven like Mahomets Paradise; and though
Ill spirits walk in white, we easly know,
By this these Angels from an evil sprite,
Those set our hairs, but these our flesh upright.
    Licence my roaving hands, and let them go,
Before, behind, between, above, below.
O my America! my new-found-land,
My kingdome, safeliest when with one man man'd,
My Myne of precious stones, My Emperie,
How blest am I in this discovering thee!
To enter in these bonds, is to be free;
Then where my hand is set, my seal shall be.

Full nakedness! All joyes are due to thee,
As souls unbodied, bodies uncloth'd must be,
To taste whole joyes. Gems which you women use
Are like Atlanta's balls, cast in mens views,
That when a fools eye lighteth on a Gem,
His earthly soul may covet theirs, not them.
Like pictures, or like books gay coverings made
For lay-men, are all women thus array'd;
Themselves are mystick books, which only wee
(Whom their imputed grace will dignifie)
Must see reveal'd. Then since that I may know;
As liberally, as to a Midwife, shew
Thy self: cast all, yea, this white lynnen hence,
There is no pennance due to innocence.

    To teach thee, I am naked first; why than
What needst thou have more covering then a man.

Elegie XX: Loves Warre

Till I have peace with thee, warr other men,
And when I have peace, can I leave thee then?
All other Warrs are scrupulous; Only thou
O fayr free Citty, maist thyselfe allowe
To any one: In Flanders, who can tell
Whether the Master presse; or men rebell?
Only we know, that which all Ideots say,
They beare most blows which come to part the fray.
France in her lunatique giddiness did hate
Ever our men, yea and our God of late;
Yet she relyes upon our Angels well,
Which nere returne; no more then they which fell.
Sick Ireland is with a strange warr possest
Like to an Ague; now raging, now at rest;
Which time will cure: yet it must doe her good
If she were purg'd, and her head vayne let blood.
And Midas joyes our Spanish journeys give,
We touch all gold, but find no food to live.
And I should be in the hott parching clyme,
To dust and ashes turn'd before my time.
To mew me in a Ship, is to inthrall
Mee in a prison, that weare like to fall;
Or in a Cloyster; save that there men dwell
In a calme heaven, here in a swaggering hell.
Long voyages are long consumptions,
And ships are carts for executions.
Yea they are Deaths; Is't not all one to flye
Into an other World, as t'is to dye?
Here let mee warr; in these armes lett mee lye;
Here lett mee parlee, batter, bleede, and dye.
Thyne armes imprison me, and myne armes thee;
Thy hart thy ransome is; take myne for mee.

Other men war that they their rest may gayne;
But wee will rest that wee may fight agayne.
Those warrs the ignorant, these th'experienc'd love,
There wee are alwayes under, here above.
There Engins farr off breed a just true feare,
Neere thrusts, pikes, stabs, yea bullets hurt not here.
There lyes are wrongs; here safe uprightly lye;
There men kill men, we'will make one by and by.
Thou nothing; I not halfe so much shall do
In these Warrs, as they may which from us two
Shall spring. Thousands wee see which travaile not
To warrs; But stay swords, armes, and shott
To make at home; And shall not I do then
More glorious service, staying to make men?

EPITHALAMIONS
OR MARRIAGE SONGS

An Epithalamion, Or mariage Song on the Lady Elizabeth, and Count Palatine being married on St Valentines day

Haile Bishop Valentine, whose day this is,
 All the Aire is thy Diocis,
  And all the chirping Choristers
And other birds are thy Parishioners,
   Thou marryest every yeare
The Lirique Larke, and the grave whispering Dove,
The Sparrow that neglects his life for love,
The household Bird, with the red stomacher,
  Thou mak'st the black bird speed as soone,
As doth the Goldfinch, or the Halcyon;
The husband cocke lookes out, and straight is sped,
And meets his wife, which brings her feather-bed.
This day more cheerfully then ever shine,
This day, which might enflame thy self, Old Valentine.

II
Till now, Thou warmd'st with multiplying loves
  Two larkes, two sparrowes, or two Doves,
   All that is nothing unto this,
For thou this day couplest two Phœnixes;

Thou mak'st a Taper see
What the sunne never saw, and what the Arke
(Which was of foules, and beasts, the cage, and park,)
Did not containe, one bed containes, through Thee,
        Two Phœnixes, whose joyned breasts
Are unto one another mutuall nests,
Where motion kindles such fires, as shall give
Yong Phœnixes, and yet the old shall live.
Whose love and courage never shall decline,
But make the whole year through, thy day, O Valentine.

III

Up then faire Phœnix Bride, frustrate the Sunne,
        Thy selfe from thine affection
        Takest warmth enough, and from thine eye
All lesser birds will take their Jollitie.
        Up, up, faire Bride, and call,
Thy starres, from out their severall boxes, take
Thy Rubies, Pearles, and Diamonds forth, and make
Thy selfe a constellation, of them All,
        And by their blazing, signifie,
That a Great Princess falls, but doth not die;
Bee thou a new starre, that to us portends
Ends of much wonder; And be Thou those ends.
Since thou dost this day in new glory shine,
May all men date Records, from this thy Valentine.

IV

Come forth, come forth, and as one glorious flame
        Meeting Another, growes the same,
        So meet thy Fredericke, and so
To an unseparable union growe.
        Since separation
Falls not on such things as are infinite,
Nor things which are but one, can disunite,

134

You'are twice inseparable, great, and one;
      Goe then to where the Bishop staies,
To make you one, his way, which divers waies
Must be effected; and when all is past,
And that you'are one, by hearts and hands made fast,
You two have one way left, your selves to'entwine,
Besides this Bishops knot, or Bishop Valentine.

V

But oh, what ailes the Sunne, that here he staies,
      Longer to day, then other daies?
      Staies he new light from these to get?
And finding here such store, is loth to set?
      And why doe you two walke,
So slowly pac'd in this procession?
Is all your care but to be look'd upon,
And be to others spectacle, and talke?
      The feast, with gluttonous delaies,
Is eaten, and too long their meat they praise,
The masquers come too late, and'I thinke, will stay,
Like Fairies, till the Cock crow them away.
Alas, did not Antiquity assigne
A night, as well as day, to thee, O Valentine?

VI

They did, and night is come; and yet wee see
      Formalities retarding thee.
      What meane these Ladies, which (as though
They were to take a clock in peeces,) goe
      So nicely about the Bride;
A Bride, before a good night could be said,
Should vanish from her cloathes, into her bed,
As Soules from bodies steale, and are not spy'd.
      But now she is laid; What though shee bee?
Yet there are more delayes, For, where is he?

135

He comes, and passes through Spheare after Spheare,
First her sheetes, then her Armes, then any where.
Let not this day, then, but this night be thine,
Thy day was but the eve to this, O Valentine.

VII

Here lyes a shee Sunne, and a hee Moone here,
  She gives the best light to his Spheare,
  Or each is both, and all, and so
They unto one another nothing owe,
  And yet they doe, but are
So just and rich in that coyne which they pay,
That neither would, nor needs forbeare, nor stay;
Neither desires to be spar'd, nor to spare,
  They quickly pay their debt, and then
Take no acquittances, but pay again;
They pay, they give, they lend, and so let fall
No such occasion to be liberall.
More truth, more courage in these two do shine,
Then all thy turtles have, and sparrows, Valentine.

VIII

And by this act of these two Phenixes
  Nature againe restored is,
  For since these two are two no more,
Ther's but one Phenix still, as was before.
  Rest now at last, and wee
As Satyres watch the Sunnes uprise, will stay
Waiting, when your eyes opened, let out day,
Onely desir'd, because your face wee see;
  Others neare you shall whispering speake,
And wagers lay, at which side day will breake,
And win by'observing, then, whose hand it is
That opens first a curtaine, hers or his;
This will be tryed to morrow after nine,
Till which houre, wee thy day enlarge, O Valentine.

Ecclogue

*Allophanes finding Idios in the country in Christmas time, repre-
hends his absence from court, at the mariage Of the Earle of
Sommerset; Idios gives an account of his purpose therein, and of
his absence thence.*

ALLOPHANES
Unseasonable man, statue of ice,
    What could to countries solitude entice
Thee, in this yeares cold and decrepit time?
    Natures instinct drawes to the warmer clime
Even small birds, who by that courage dare,
    In numerous fleets, saile through their Sea, the aire.
What delicacie can in fields appeare,
    Whil'st Flora'herselfe doth a freeze jerkin weare?
Whil'st windes do all the trees and hedges strip
    Of leafes, to furnish roddes enough to whip
Thy madnesse from thee; and all springs by frost
    Have taken cold, and their sweet murmures lost;
If thou thy faults or fortunes would'st lament
    With just solemnity, do it in Lent;
At Court the spring already advanced is,
    The Sunne stayes longer up; and yet not his
The glory is, farre other, other fires.
    First, zeale to Prince and State; then loves desires
Burne in one brest, and like heavens two great lights,
    The first doth governe dayes, the other nights.
And then that early light, which did appeare
    Before the Sunne and Moone created were,
The Princes favour is defused o'r all,
    From which all Fortunes, Names, and Natures fall;

Then from those wombes of starres, the Brides bright eyes,
    At every glance, a constellation flyes,
And sowes the Court with starres, and doth prevent
    In light and power, the all-ey'd firmament;
First her eyes kindle other Ladies eyes,
    Then from their beames their jewels lusters rise,
And from their jewels torches do take fire,
    And all is warmth, and light, and good desire;
Most other Courts, alas, are like to hell,
    Where in darke plotts, fire without light doth dwell:
Or but like Stoves, for lust and envy get
    Continuall, but artificiall heat;
Here zeale and love growne one, all clouds disgest,
    And make our Court an everlasting East.
And can'st thou be from thence?

IDIOS   No, I am there.
    As heaven, to men dispos'd, is every where,
So are those Courts, whose Princes animate,
    Not onely all their house, but all their State.
Let no man thinke, because he is full, he hath all,
    Kings (as their patterne, God) are liberall
Not onely in fulnesse, but capacitie,
    Enlarging narrow men, to feele and see,
And comprehend the blessings they bestow.
    So, reclus'd hermits often times do know
More of heavens glory, then a worldling can.
    As man is of the world, the heart of man,
Is an epitome of Gods great booke
    Of creatures, and man need no farther looke;
So is the Country of Courts, where sweet peace doth,
    As their one common soule, give life to both,
I am not then from Court.

ALLOPHANES   Dreamer, thou art.
 Think'st thou fantastique that thou hast a part
In the East-Indian fleet, because thou hast
 A little spice, or Amber in thy taste?
Because thou art not frozen, art thou warme?
 Seest thou all good because thou seest no harme?
The earth doth in her inward bowels hold
 Stuffe well dispos'd, and which would faine be gold,
But never shall, except it chance to lye,
 So upward, that heaven gild it with his eye;
As, for divine things, faith comes from above,
 So, for best civil use, all tinctures move
From higher powers; From God religion springs,
 Wisdome, and honour from the use of Kings.
Then unbeguile thy selfe, and know with mee,
 That Angels, though on earth employd they bee,
Are still in heav'n, so is hee still at home
 That doth, abroad, to honest actions come.
Chide thy selfe then, O foole, which yesterday
 Might'st have read more then all thy books bewray;
Hast thou a history, which doth present
 A Court, where all affections do assent
Unto the Kings, and that, that Kings are just?
 And where it is no levity to trust?
Where there is no ambition, but to'obey,
 Where men need whisper nothing, and yet may;
Where the Kings favours are so plac'd, that all
 Finde that the King therein is liberall
To them, in him, because his favours bend
 To vertue, to the which they all pretend?
Thou hast no such; yet here was this, and more,
 An earnest lover, wise then, and before.

Our little Cupid hath sued Livery,
    And is no more in his minority,
Hee is admitted now into that brest
    Where the Kings Counsells and his secrets rest.
What has thou lost, O ignorant man?

IDIOS   I knew
    All this, and onely therefore I withdrew.
To know and feele all this, and not to have
    Words to expresse it, makes a man a grave
Of his owne thoughts; I would not therefore stay
    At a great feast, having no Grace to say.
And yet I scap'd not here; for being come
    Full of the common joy, I utter'd some;
Reade then this nuptiall song, which was not made
    Either the Court or mens hearts to invade,
But since I'am dead, and buried, I could frame
    No Epitaph, which might advance my fame
So much as this poore song, which testifies
    I did unto that day some sacrifice.

Epithalamion

I: The Time of the Mariage

Thou art repriv'd old yeare, thou shalt not die,
    Though thou upon thy death bed lye,
    And should'st within five dayes expire,
Yet thou art rescu'd by a mightier fire,
    Then thy old Soule, the Sunne,
When he doth in his largest circle runne.
The passage of the West or East would thaw,
And open wide their easie liquid jawe
To all our ships, could a Promethean art
Either unto the Northerne Pole impart
The fire of these inflaming eyes, or of this loving heart.

II: Equality of persons

But undiscerning Muse, which heart, which eyes,
    In this new couple, dost thou prize,
    When his eyes as inflaming is
As hers, and her heart loves as well as his?
    Be tryed by beauty, and than
The bridegroome is a maid, and not a man.
If by that manly courage they be tryed,
Which scornes unjust opinion; then the bride
Becomes a man. Should chance or envies Art
Divide these two, whom nature scarce did part?
Since both have both th'enflaming eyes, and both the loving
    heart.

III: Raysing of the Bridegroome

Though it be some divorce to thinke of you
    Singly, so much one are you two,
    Yet let me here contemplate thee,
First, cheerfull Bridegroome, and first let mee see,

How thou prevent'st the Sunne,
And his red foming horses dost outrunne,
How, having laid downe in thy Soveraignes brest
All businesses, from thence to reinvest
Them, when these triumphs cease, thou forward art
To shew to her, who doth the like impart,
The fire of thy inflaming eyes, and of thy loving heart.

IV : Raising of the Bride

But now, to Thee, faire Bride, it is some wrong,
To thinke thou wert in Bed so long,
Since Soone thou lyest downe first, 'tis fit
Thou in first rising should'st allow for it.
Pouder thy Radiant haire,
Which if without such ashes thou would'st weare,
Thou, which to all which come to looke upon,
Art meant for Phœbus, would'st be Phaëton.
For our ease, give thine eyes th'unusual part
Of joy, a Teare; so quencht, thou maist impart,
To us that come, thy inflaming eyes, to him, thy loving
heart.

V : Her Apparrelling

Thus thou descend'st to our infirmitie,
Who can the Sun in water see.
Soe dost thou, when in silke and gold,
Thou cloudst thy selfe; since wee which doe behold,
Are dust, and wormes, 'tis just
Our objects be the fruits of wormes and dust;
Let every Jewell be a glorious starre,
Yet starres are not so pure, as their spheares are.
And though thou stoope, to'appeare to us in part,
Still in that Picture thou intirely art,
Which thy inflaming eyes have made within his loving
heart.

VI: Going to the Chappell

Now from your Easts you issue forth, and wee,
    As men which through a Cipres see
    The rising sun, doe thinke it two,
Soe, as you goe to Church, doe thinke of you,
    But that vaile being gone,
By the Church rites you are from thenceforth one.
The Church Triumphant made this match before,
And now the Militant doth strive no more;
Then, reverend Priest, who Gods Recorder art,
Doe, from his Dictates, to these two impart
All blessings, which are seene, or thought, by Angels eye
    or heart.

VII: The Benediction

Blest payre of Swans, Oh may you interbring
    Daily new joyes, and never sing,
    Live, till all grounds of wishes faile,
Till honor, yea till wisedome grow so stale,
    That, new great heights to trie,
It must serve your ambition, to die;
Raise heires, and may here, to the worlds end, live
Heires from this King, to take thankes, you, to give,
Nature and grace doe all, and nothing Art.
May never age, or error overthwart
With any West, these radiant eyes, with any North, this
    heart.

VIII: Feasts and Revells

But you are over-blest. Plenty this day
    Injures; it causeth time to stay;
    The tables groane, as though this feast
Would, as the flood, destroy all fowle and beast.

And were the doctrine new
That the earth mov'd, this day would make it true;
For every part to dance and revell goes.
They tread the ayre, and fal not where they rose.
Though six houres since, the Sunne to bed did part,
The masks and banquets will not yet impart
A sunset to these weary eyes, A Center to this heart.

IX: *The Brides going to bed*

What mean'st thou Bride, this companie to keep?
    To sit up, till thou faine wouldst sleep?
    Thou maist not, when thou art laid, doe so.
Thy selfe must to him a new banquet grow,
    And you must entertaine
And doe all this daies dances o'r againe.
Know that if Sun and Moone together doe
Rise in one point, they doe not set so too;
Therefore thou maist, faire Bride, to bed depart,
Thou art not gone, being gone; where e'r thou art,
Thou leav'st in him thy watchfull eyes, in him thy loving
    heart.

X: *The Bridegroomes comming*

As he that sees a starre fall, runs apace,
    And findes a gellie in the place,
    So doth the Bridegroome hast as much,
Being told this starre is falne, and findes her such.
    And as friends may looke strange,
By a new fashion, or apparrells change,
Their soules, though long acquainted they had beene,
These clothes, their bodies, never yet had seene;
Therefore at first shee modestly might start,
But must forthwith surrender every part,
As freely, as each to each before, gave either eye or heart.

XI: *The good-night*

Now, as in Tullias tombe, one lampe burnt cleare,
    Unchang'd for fifteene hundred yeare,
    May these love-lamps we here enshrine,
In warmth, light, lasting, equall the divine.
      Fire ever doth aspire,
And makes all like it selfe, turnes all to fire,
But ends in ashes, which these cannot doe,
For none of these is fuell, but fire too.
This is joyes bonfire, then, where loves strong Arts
Make of so noble individuall parts
One fire of foure inflaming eyes, and of two loving hearts.
   IDIOS
As I have brought this song, that I may doe
    A perfect sacrifice, I'll burne it too.
   ALLOPHANES
No S^r. This paper I have justly got,
  For, in burnt incense, the perfume is not
His only that presents it, but of all;
    What ever celebrates this Festivall
Is common, since the joy thereof is so.
  Nor may your selfe be Priest: But let me goe,
Backe to the Court, and I will lay'it upon
  Such Altars, as prize your devotion.

Epithalamion made at Lincolnes Inne

The Sun-beames in the East are spred,
Leave, leave, faire Bride, your solitary bed,
  No more shall you returne to it alone,
It nourseth sadnesse, and your bodies print,
Like to a grave, the yielding downe doth dint;
    You and your other you meet there anon;
    Put forth, put forth that warme balme-breathing thigh,
Which when next time you in these sheets wil smother,
    There it must meet another,
      Which never was, but must be, oft, more nigh;
Come glad from thence, goe gladder then you came,
To day put on perfection, and a womans name.

Daughters of London, you which bee
Our Golden Mines, and furnish'd Treasurie,
  You which are Angels, yet still bring with you
Thousands of Angels on your mariage daies,
Help with your presence and devise to praise
    These rites, which also unto you grow due;
    Conceitedly dresse her, and be assign'd,
By you, fit place for very flower and jewell,
    Make her for love fit fewell
      As gay as Flora, and as rich as Inde;
So may shee faire, rich, glad, and in nothing lame,
To day put on perfection, and a womans name.

And you frolique Patricians,
Sonnes of these Senators, wealths deep oceans,
  Ye painted courtiers, barrels of others wits,
Yee country men, who but your beasts love none,
Yee of those fellowships whereof hee's one,

Of study and play made strange Hermaphrodits,
　　Here shine; This Bridegroom to the Temple bring.
Loe, in yon path which store of straw'd flowers graceth,
　　The sober virgin paceth;
　　　Except my sight faile, 'tis no other thing;
Weep not nor blush, here is no griefe nor shame,
To day put on perfection, and a womans name.

Thy two-leav'd gates faire Temple unfold,
And these two in thy sacred bosome hold,
　　Till, mystically joyn'd, but one they bee;
Then may thy leane and hunger-starved wombe
Long time expect their bodies and their tombe,
　　Long after their owne parents fatten thee.
　　All elder claimes, and all cold barrennesse,
All yeelding to new loves bee far for ever,
　　Which might these two dissever,
　　　All wayes all th'other may each one possesse;
For, the best Bride, best worthy of praise and fame,
To day puts on perfection, and a womans name.

Oh winter dayes bring much delight,
Not for themselves, but for they soon bring night;
　　Other sweets wait thee then these diverse meats,
Other disports then dancing jollities,
Other love tricks then glancing with the eyes,
　　But that the Sun still in our halfe Spheare sweates;
　　　Hee flies in winter, but he now stands still.
Yet shadowes turne; Noone point he hath attain'd,
　　He steeds nill bee restrain'd,
　　　But gallop lively downe the Westerne hill;
Thou shalt, when he hath runne the worlds half frame,
To night put on perfection, and a womans name.

The amorous evening starre is rose,
Why then should not our amorous starre inclose
   Her self in her wish'd bed? Release your strings
Musicians, and dancers take some truce
With these your pleasing labours, for great use
    As much wearinesse as perfection brings;
      You, and not only you, but all toyl'd beasts
Rest duly; at night all their toyles are dispensed;
But in their beds commenced
      Are other labours, and more dainty feasts;
She goes a maid, who, least she turne the same,
To night puts on perfection, and a womans name.

Thy virgins girdle now untie,
And in thy nuptiall bed (loves altar) lye
   A pleasing sacrifice; now dispossesse
Thee of these chaines and robes which were put on
T'adorne the day, not thee; for thou, alone,
    Like vertue'and truth, are best in nakednesse;
      This bed is onely to virginitie
A grave, but, to a better state, a cradle;
Till now thou wast but able
    To be what now thou art; then that by thee
No more be said, *I may be*, but, *I am*,
To night put on perfection, and a womans name.

Even like a faithfull man content,
That this life for a better should be spent,
   So, shee a mothers rich stile doth preferre,
And at the Bridegroomes wish'd approach doth lye,
Like an appointed lambe, when tenderly

The priest comes on his knees t'embowell her;
    Now sleep or watch with more joy; and O light
Of heaven, to morrow rise thou hot, and early;
This Sun will love so dearely
    Her rest, that long, long we shall want her sight;
Wonders are wrought, for shee which had no maime,
To night puts on perfection, and a womans name.

DIVINE POEMS

To E of D with six holy Sonnets

See Sir, how as the Suns hot Masculine flame
Begets strange creatures on Niles durty slime,
  In me, your fatherly yet lusty Ryme
(For, these songs are their fruits) have wrought the same;
But though the ingendring force from whence they came
  Bee strong enough, and nature doe admit
  Seaven to be borne at once, I send as yet
But six; they say, the seaventh hath still some maime.
  I choose your judgement, which the same degree
  Doth with her sister, your invention, hold,
As fire these drossie Rymes to purifie,
  Or as Elixar, to change them to gold;
You are that Alchimist which alwaies had
Wit, whose one spark could make good things of bad.

To the Lady Magdalen Herbert:
of St Mary Magdalen

Her of your name, whose fair inheritance
 Bethina was, and jointure Magdalo:
An active faith so highly did advance,
 That she once knew, more than the Church did know,
The Resurrection; so much good there is
 Deliver'd of her, that some Fathers be
Loth to believe one Woman could do this;
 But, think these Magdalens were two or three.
Increase their number, Lady, and their fame:
 To their Devotion, add your Innocence;
Take so much of th'example, as of the name;
 The latter half; and in some recompence
That they did harbour Christ himself, a Guest,
 Harbour these Hymns, to his dear name addrest. J.D.

HOLY SONNETS

I: *La Corona*

Deigne at my hands this crown of prayer and praise,
Weav'd in my low devout melancholie,
Thou which of good, hast, yea art treasury,
All changing unchang'd Antient of dayes;
But doe not, with a vile crowne of fraile bayes,
Reward my muses white sincerity,
But what thy thorny crowne gain'd, that give mee,
A crowne of Glory, which doth flower alwayes;
The ends crowne our workes, but thou crown'st our ends,
For, at our end begins our endlesse rest;
The first last end, now zealously possest,
With a strong sober thirst, my soule attends.
'Tis time that heart and voice be lifted high,
Salvation to all that will is nigh.

II: *Annunciation*

Salvation to all that will is nigh;
That All, which alwayes is All every where,
Which cannot sinne, and yet all sinnes must beare,
Which cannot die, yet cannot chuse but die,
Loe, faithfull Virgin, yeelds himselfe to lye
In prison, in thy wombe; and though he there
Can take no sinne, nor thou give, yet he'will weare
Taken from thence, flesh, which deaths force may trie.
Ere by the spheares time was created, thou
Wast in his minde, who is thy Sonne, and Brother;
Whom thou conceiv'st, conceiv'd; yea thou art now
Thy Makers maker, and thy Fathers mother;
Thou'hast light in darke; and shutst in little roome,
Immensity cloysterd in thy deare wombe.

III: Nativitie

Immensitie cloysterd in thy deare wombe,
Now leaves his welbelov'd imprisonment,
There he hath made himselfe to his intent
Weake enough, now into our world to come;
But Oh, for thee, for him, hath th'Inne no roome?
Yet lay him in this stall, and from the Orient,
Starres, and wisemen will travell to prevent
Th'effect of *Herods* jealous generall doome.
Seest thou, my Soule, with thy faiths eyes, how he
Which fils all place, yet none holds him, doth lye?
Was not his pity towards thee wondrous high,
That would have need to be pittied by thee?
Kisse him, and with him into Egypt goe,
With his kinde mother, who partakes thy woe.

IV: Temple

With his kinde mother who partakes thy woe,
Joseph turne backe; see where your child doth sit,
Blowing, yea blowing out those sparks of wit,
Which himselfe on the Doctors did bestow;
The Word but lately could not speake, and loe,
It sodenly speakes wonders, whence comes it,
That all which was, and all which should be writ,
A shallow seeming child, should deeply know?
His Godhead was not soule to his manhood,
Nor had time mellowed him to this ripenesse,
But as for one which hath a long taske, 'tis good,
With the Sunne to beginne his businesse,
He in his ages morning thus began
By miracles exceeding power of man.

V: Crucifying

By miracles exceeding power of man,
Hee faith in some, envie in some begat,
For, what weake spirits admire, ambitious, hate
In both affections many to him ran,
But Oh! the worst are most, they will and can,
Alas, and do, unto the immaculate,
Whose creature Fate is, now prescribe a Fate,
Measuring selfe-lifes infinity to'a span,
Nay to an inch. Loe, where condemned hee
Beares his owne crosse, with paine, yet by and by
When it beares him, he must beare more and die.
Now thou art lifted up, draw mee to thee,
And at thy death giving such liberall dole,
Moyst, with one drop of thy blood, my dry soule.

VI: Resurrection

Moyst with one drop of thy blood, my dry soule
Shall (though she now be in extreme degree
Too stony hard, and yet too fleshly,) bee
Freed by that drop, from being starv'd, hard, or foule,
And life, by this death abled, shall controule
Death, whom thy death slue; nor shall to mee
Feare of first or last death, bring miserie,
If in thy little booke my name thou enroule,
Flesh in that long sleep is not putrified,
But made that there, of which, and for which 'twas;
Nor can by other meanes be glorified.
May then sinnes sleep, and deaths soone from me passe,
That wak't from both, I againe risen may
Salute the last, and everlasting day.

VII: Ascension

Salute the last and everlasting day,
Joy at the uprising of this Sunne, and Sonne,
Yee whose just teares, or tribulation
Have purely washt, or burnt your drossie clay;
Behold the Highest, parting hence away,
Lightens the darke clouds, which hee treads upon,
Nor doth hee by ascending, show alone,
But first hee, and hee first enters the way.
O strong Ramme, which hast batter'd heaven for mee,
Mild Lambe, which with thy blood, hast mark'd the path;
Bright Torch, which shin'st, that I the way may see,
Oh, with thy owne blood quench thy owne just wrath,
And if thy holy Spirit, my Muse did raise,
Deigne at my hands this crowne of prayer and praise.

Holy Sonnets

I

Thou hast made me, And shall thy worke decay?
Repaire me now, for now mine end doth haste,
I runne to death, and death meets me as fast,
And all my pleasures are like yesterday;
I dare not move my dimme eyes any way,
Despaire behind, and death before doth cast
Such terrour, and my feebled flesh doth waste
By sinne in it, which it t'wards hell doth weigh;
Onely thou art above, and when towards thee
By thy leave I can looke, I rise againe;
But our old subtle foe so tempteth me,
That not one houre my selfe I can sustaine;
Thy Grace may wing me to prevent his art,
And thou like Adamant draw mine iron heart.

II

As due by many titles I resigne
My selfe to thee, O God, first I was made
By thee, and for thee, and when I was decay'd
Thy blood bought that, the which before was thine;
I am thy sonne, made with thy selfe to shine,
Thy servant, whose paines thou hast still repaid,
Thy sheepe, thine Image, and, till I betray'd
My selfe, a temple of thy Spirit divine;
Why doth the devill then usurpe on mee?
Why doth he steale, nay ravish that's thy right?
Except thou rise and for thine owne worke fight,
Oh I shall soone despaire, when I doe see
That thou lov'st mankind well, yet wilt'not chuse me.
And Satan hates mee, yet is loth to lose mee.

III

O might those sighes and teares returne againe
Into my breast and eyes, which I have spent,
That I might in this holy discontent
Mourne with some fruit, as I have mourn'd in vaine;
In mine Idolatry what showres of raine
Mine eyes did waste? what griefs my heart did rent?
That sufferance was my sinne; now I repent;
'Cause I did suffer I must suffer paine.
Th'hydroptique drunkard, and night-scouting thiefe,
The itchy Lecher, and selfe tickling proud
Have the remembrance of past joyes, for reliefe
Of comming ills. To (poore) me is allow'd
No ease; for, long, yet vehement griefe hath beene
Th'effect and cause, the punishment and sinne.

IV

Oh my blacke Soule! now thou art summoned
By sicknesse, deaths herald, and champion;
Thou art like a pilgrim, which abroad hath done
Treason, and durst not turne to whence hee is fled,
Or like a thiefe, which till deaths doome be read,
Wisheth himselfe delivered from prison;
But damn'd and hal'd to execution,
Wisheth that still he might be imprisoned.
Yet grace, if thou repent, thou canst not lacke;
But who shall give thee that grace to beginne?
Oh make thy selfe with holy mourning blacke,
And red with blushing, as thou art with sinne;
Or wash thee in Christs blood, which hath this might
That being red, it dyes red soules to white.

V

I am a little world made cunningly
Of Elements, and an Angelike spright,
But black sinne hath betraid to endlesse night
My worlds both parts, and (oh) both parts must die.
You which beyond that heaven which was most high
Have found new sphears, and of new lands can write,
Powre new seas in mine eyes, that so I might
Drowne my world with my weeping earnestly,
Or wash it, if it must be drown'd no more:
But oh it must be burnt! alas the fire
Of lust and envie have burnt it heretofore,
And made it fouler; Let their flames retire,
And burne me ô Lord, with a fiery zeale
Of thee and thy house, which doth in eating heale.

VI

This is my playes last scene, here heavens appoint
My pilgrimages last mile; and my race
Idly, yet quickly runne, hath this last pace,
My spans last inch, my minutes latest point,
And gluttonous death, will instantly unjoynt
My body, and soule, and I shall sleepe a space,
But my'ever-waking part shall see that face,
Whose feare already shakes my every joynt:
Then, as my soule, to'heaven her first seate, takes flight,
And earth-borne body, in the earth shall dwell,
So, fall my sinnes, that all may have their right,
To where they'are bred, and would presse me, to hell.
Impute me righteous, thus purg'd of evill,
For thus I leave the world, the flesh, the devill.

VII

At the round earths imagin'd corners, blow
Your trumpets, Angells, and arise, arise
From death, you numberlesse infinities
Of soules, and to your scattred bodies goe,
All whom the flood did, and fire shall o'erthrow,
All whom warre, dearth, age, agues, tyrannies,
Despaire, law, chance, hath slaine, and you whose eyes,
Shall behold God, and never tast deaths woe.
But let them sleepe, Lord, and mee mourne a space,
For, if above all these, my sinnes abound,
'Tis late to aske abundance of thy grace,
When wee are there; here on this lowly ground,
Teach mee how to repent; for that's as good
As if thou'hadst seal'd my pardon, with thy blood.

VIII

If faithfull soules be alike glorifi'd
As Angels, then my fathers soule doth see,
And adds this even to full felicitie,
That valiantly I hels wide mouth o'rstride:
But if our mindes to these soules be descry'd
By circumstances, and by signes that be
Apparent in us, not immediately,
How shall my mindes white truth by them be try'd?
They see idolatrous lovers weepe and mourne,
And vile blasphemous Conjurers to call
On Jesus name, and Pharisaicall
Dissemblers feigne devotion. Then turne
O pensive soule, to God, for he knowes best
Thy true griefe, for he put it in my breast.

IX

If poysonous mineralls, and if that tree,
Whose fruit threw death on else immortall us,
If lecherous goats, if serpents envious
Cannot be damn'd; Alas; why should I bee?
Why should intent or reason, borne in mee,
Make sinnes, else equall, in mee more heinous?
And mercy being easie, and glorious
To God; in his sterne wrath, why threatens hee?
But who am I, that dare dispute with thee
O God? Oh! of thine onely worthy blood,
And my teares, make a heavenly Lethean flood,
And drowne in it my sinnes blacke memorie;
That thou remember them, some claime as debt,
I think it mercy, if thou wilt forget.

X

Death be not proud, though some have called thee
Mighty and dreadfull, for, thou art not soe,
For, those, whom thou think'st, thou dost overthrow,
Die not, poore death, nor yet canst thou kill mee.
From rest and sleepe, which but thy pictures bee,
Much pleasure, then from thee, much more must flow,
And soonest our best men with thee doe goe,
Rest of their bones, and soules deliverie.
Thou art slave to Fate, Chance, kings, and desperate men,
And dost with poyson, warre, and sicknesse dwell,
And poppie, or charmes can make us sleepe as well,
And better then thy stroake; why swell'st thou then?
One short sleepe past, wee wake eternally,
And death shall be no more; death, thou shalt die.

XI

Spit in my face, you Jewes, and pierce my side,
Buffet, and scoffe, scourge, and crucifie mee,
For I have sinn'd, and sinn'd, and onely hee,
Who could do no iniquitie, hath dyed:
But by my death can not be satisfied
My sinnes, which passe the Jewes impiety:
They kill'd once an inglorious man, but I
Crucifie him daily, being now glorified.
Oh let mee then, his strange love still admire:
Kings pardon, but he bore our punishment.
And *Jacob* came cloth'd in vile harsh attire
But to supplant, and with gainfull intent:
　　God cloth'd himselfe in vile mans flesh, that so
　　Hee might be weake enough to suffer woe.

XII

Why are wee by all creatures waited on?
Why doe the prodigall elements supply
Life and food to mee, being more pure then I,
Simple, and further from corruption?
Why brook'st thou, ignorant horse, subjection?
Why dost thou bull, and bore so seelily
Dissemble weaknesse, and by'one mans stroke die,
Whose whole kinde, you might swallow and feed upon?
Weaker I am, woe is mee, and worse then you,
You have not sinn'd, nor need be timorous.
But wonder at a greater wonder, for to us
Created nature doth these things subdue,
But their Creator, whom sin, nor nature tyed,
For us, his Creatures, and his foes, hath dyed.

XIII

What if this present were the worlds last night?
Marke in my heart, O Soule, where thou dost dwell,
The picture of Christ crucified, and tell
Whether that countenance can thee affright,
Teares in his eyes quench the amasing light,
Blood fills his frownes, which from his pierc'd head fell.
And can that tongue adjudge thee unto hell,
Which pray'd forgivenesse for his foes fierce spight?
No, no; but as in my idolatrie
I said to all my profane mistresses,
Beauty, of pitty, foulnesse onely is
A signe of rigour: so I say to thee,
To wicked spirits are horrid shapes assign'd,
This beauteous forme assures a pitious minde.

XIV

Batter my heart, three person'd God; for, you
As yet but knocke, breathe, shine, and seeke to mend;
That I may rise, and stand, o'erthrow mee,'and bend
Your force, to breake, blowe, burn and make me new.
I, like an usurpt towne, to'another due,
Labour to'admit you, but Oh, to no end,
Reason your viceroy in mee, mee should defend,
But is captiv'd, and proves weake or untrue.
Yet dearely'I love you,'and would be loved faine,
But am betroth'd unto your enemie:
Divorce mee,'untie, or breake that knot againe,
Take mee to you, imprison mee, for I
Except you'enthrall mee, never shall be free,
Nor ever chast, except you ravish mee.

XV

Wilt thou love God, as he thee! then digest,
My Soule, this wholsome meditation,
How God the Spirit, by Angels waited on
In heaven, doth make his Temple in thy brest.
The Father having begot a Sonne most blest,
And still begetting, (for he ne'r begonne)
Hath deign'd to chuse thee by adoption,
Coheire to'his glory,'and Sabbaths endlesse rest.
And as a robb'd man, which by search doth finde
His stolne stuffe sold, must lose or buy'it againe:
The Sonne of glory came downe, and was slaine,
Us whom he'had made, and Satan stolne, to unbinde.
'Twas much, that man was made like God before,
But, that God should be made like man, much more.

XVI

Father, part of his double interest
Unto thy kingdome, thy Sonne gives to mee,
His joynture in the knottie Trinitie
Hee keepes, and gives to me his deaths conquest.
This Lambe, whose death, with life the world hath blest,
Was from the worlds beginning slaine, and he
Hath made two Wills, which with the Legacie
Of his and thy kingdome, doe thy Sonnes invest.
Yet such are thy laws, that men argue yet
Whether a man those statutes can fulfill;
None doth; but all-healing grace and spirit
Revive againe what law and letter kill.
Thy lawes abridgement, and thy last command
Is all but love; Oh let this last Will stand!

Since she whom I lov'd hath payd her last debt
To Nature, and to hers, and my good is dead,
And her Soule early into heaven ravished,
Wholly on heavenly things my mind is sett.
Here the admyring her my mind did whett
To seeke thee God; so streames do shew their head;
But though I have found thee, and thou my thirst hast fed,
A holy thirsty dropsy melts mee yett.
But why should I begg more Love, when as thou
Dost wooe my soule for hers; offring all thine:
And dost not only fear least I allow
My Love to Saints and Angels, things divine,
But in thy tender jealosy dost doubt
Least the World, Fleshe, yea Devill putt thee out.

Show me deare Christ, thy spouse, so bright and clear.
What! is it She, which on the other shore
Goes richly painted? or which rob'd and tore
Laments and mournes in Germany and here?
Sleepes she a thousand, then peepes up one yeare?
Is she selfe truth and errs? now new, now outwore?
Doth she, and did she, and shall she evermore
On one, on seaven, or on no hill appeare?
Dwells she with us, or like adventuring knights
First travaile we to seeke and then make Love?
Betray kind husband thy spouse to our sights,
And let myne amorous soule court thy mild Dove,
Who is most trew, and pleasing to thee, then
When she'is embrac'd and open to most men.

XIX

Oh, to vex me, contraryes meet in one:
Inconstancy unnaturally hath begott
A constant habit; that when I would not
I change in vowes, and in devotione.
As humorous is my contritione
As my prophane Love, and as soone forgott:
As ridlingly distemper'd, cold and hott,
As praying, as mute; as infinite, as none.
I durst not view heaven yesterday; and to day
In prayers, and flattering speaches I court God:
To morrow I quake with true feare of his rod.
So my devout fitts come and go away
Like a fantastique Ague: save that here
Those are my best dayes, when I shake with feare.

The Crosse

Since Christ embrac'd the Crosse it selfe, dare I
His image, th'image of his Crosse deny?
Would I have profit by the sacrifice,
And dare the chosen Altar to despise?
It bore all other sinnes, but is it fit
That it should beare the sinne of scorning it?
Who from the picture would avert his eye,
How would he flye his paines, who there did dye?
From mee, no Pulpit, nor misgrounded law,
Nor scandall taken, shall this Cross withdraw,
It shall not, for it cannot; for, the losse
Of this Crosse, were to mee another Crosse;
Better were worse, for, no affliction,
No Crosse is so extreme, as to have none.
Who can blot out the Crosse, which th'instrument
Of God, dew'd on mee in the Sacrament?
Who can deny mee power, and liberty
To stretch mine armes, and mine owne Crosse to be?
Swimme, and at every stroake, thou art thy Crosse;
The Mast and yard make one, where seas do tosse;
Looke downe, thou spiest out Crosses in small things;
Looke up, thou seest birds rais'd on crossed wings;
All the Globes frame, and spheares, is nothing else
But the Meridians crossing Parallels.
Materiall Crosses then, good physicke bee,
But yet spirituall have chiefe dignity.
These for extracted chimique medicine serve,
And cure much better, and as well preserve;
Then are you your own physicke, or need none,
When Still'd, or purg'd by tribulation.
For when that Crosse ungrudg'd, unto you stickes,
Then are you to your selfe, a Crucifixe.
As perchance, Carvers do not faces make,
But that away, which hid them there, do take;

Let Crosses, soe, take what hid Christ in thee,
And be his image, or not his, but hee.
But, as oft Alchimists doe coyners prove,
So may a selfe-dispising, get selfe-love,
And then as worst surfets, of best meates bee,
Soe is pride, issued from humility,
For, 'tis no child, but monster; therefore Crosse
Your joy in crosses, else, 'tis double losse.
And crosse thy senses, else, both they, and thou
Must perish soone, and to destruction bowe.
For if the'eye seeke good objects, and will take
No crosse from bad, wee cannot scape a snake.
So with harsh, hard, sowre, stinking, crosse the rest,
Make them indifferent all; call nothing best.
But most the eye needs crossing, that can rome,
And move; To th'other th'objects must come home.
And crosse thy heart: for that in man alone
Points downewards, and hath palpitation.
Crosse those dejections, when it downeward tends,
And when it to forbidden heights pretends.
And as the braine through bony walls doth vent
By sutures, which a Crosses forme present,
So when thy braine workes, ere thou utter it,
Crosse and correct concupiscence of witt.
Be covetous of Crosses, let none fall.
Crosse no man else, but crosse thy selfe in all.
Then doth the Crosse of Christ worke fruitfully
Within our hearts, when wee love harmlessly
That Crosses pictures much, and with more care
That Crosses children, which our Crosses are.

Resurrection, imperfect

Sleep sleep old Sun, thou canst not have repast
As yet, the wound thou took'st on friday last;
Sleepe then, and rest; The world may beare thy stay,
A better Sun rose before thee to day,
Who, not content to'enlighten all that dwell
On the earths face, as thou, enlightned hell,
And made the darke fires languish in that vale,
As, at thy presence here, our fires grow pale.
Whose body having walk'd on earth, and now
Hasting to Heaven, would, that he might allow
Himselfe unto all stations, and fill all,
For these three daies become a minerall;
Hee was all gold when he lay downe, but rose
All tincture, and doth not alone dispose
Leaden and iron wills to good, but is
Of power to make even sinfull flesh like this.
Had one of those, whose credulous pietie
Thought, that a Soule one might discerne and see
Goe from a body,'at this sepulcher been,
And, issuing from the sheet, this body seen,
He would have justly thought this body a soule,
If not of any man, yet of the whole.

Desunt cætera

The Annunciation and Passion

Tamely, fraile body,'abstaine to day; to day
My soule eates twice, Christ hither and away.
Shee sees him man, so like God made in this,
That of them both a circle embleme is,
Whose first and last concurre; this doubtfull day
Of feast or fast, Christ came, and went away.
Shee sees him nothing twice at once, who'is all;
Shee sees a Cedar plant it selfe, and fall,
Her Maker put to making, and the head
Of life, at once, not yet alive, yet dead.
She sees at once the virgin mother stay
Reclus'd at home, Publique at Golgotha;
Sad and rejoyc'd shee's seen at once, and seen
At almost fiftie, and at scarce fifteene.
At once a Sonne is promis'd her, and gone,
Gabriell gives Christ to her, He her to John;
Not fully a mother, Shee's in Orbitie,
At once receiver and the legacie.
All this, and all betweene, this day hath showne,
The' Abridgement of Christs story, which makes one
(As in plaine Maps, the furthest West is East)
Of the'Angels *Ave,*'and *Consummatum est.*
How well the Church, Gods Court of faculties
Deales, in some times, and seldome joyning these!
As by the selfe-fix'd Pole wee never doe
Direct our course, but the next starre thereto,
Which showes where the'other is, and which we say
(Because it strayes not farre) doth never stray;
So God by his Church, neerest to him, wee know,
And stand firme, if wee by her motion goe;
His Spirit, as his fiery Pillar doth
Leade, and his Church, as cloud; to one end both.

This Church, by letting these daies joyne, hath shown
Death and conception in mankinde is one;
Or 'twas in him the same humility,
That he would be a man, and leave to be:
Or as creation he hath made, as God,
With the last judgement, but one period,
His imitating Spouse would joyne in one
Manhoods extremes: He shall come, he is gone:
Or as though one blood drop, which thence did fall,
Accepted, would have serv'd, he yet shed all;
So though the least of his paines, deeds, or words,
Would busie a life, she all this day affords;
This treasure then, in grosse, my Soule uplay,
And in my life retaile it every day.

Goodfriday, 1613. Riding Westward

Let mans Soule be a Spheare, and then, in this,
The intelligence that moves, devotion is,
And as the other Spheares, by being growne
Subject to forraigne motions, lose their owne,
And being by others hurried every day,
Scarce in a yeare their naturall forme obey:
Pleasure or businesse, so, our Soules admit
For their first mover, and are whirld by it.
Hence is't, that I am carryed towards the West
This day, when my Soules forme bends toward the East.
There I should see a Sunne, by rising set,
And by that setting endlesse day beget;
But that Christ on this Crosse, did rise and fall,
Sinne had eternally benighted all.
Yet dare I'almost be glad, I do not see
That spectacle of too much weight for mee.
Who sees Gods face, that is selfe life, must dye;
What a death were it then to see God dye?
It made his owne Lieutenant Nature shrinke,
It made his footstoole crack, and the Sunne winke.
Could I behold those hands which span the Poles,
And turne all spheares at once, pierc'd with those holes?
Could I behold that endlesse height which is
Zenith to us, and our Antipodes,
Humbled below us? or that blood which is
The seat of all our Soules, if not of his,
Made durt of dust, or that flesh which was worne
By God, for his apparell, rag'd, and torne?
If on these things I durst not looke, durst I
Upon his miserable mother cast mine eye,
Who was Gods partner here, and furnish'd thus
Halfe of that Sacrifice, which ransom'd us?

Though these things, as I ride, be from mine eye,
They'are present yet unto my memory,
For that looks towards them; and thou look'st towards
O Saviour, as thou hang'st upon the tree;   [mee,
I turne my backe to thee, but to receive
Corrections, till thy mercies bid thee leave.
O thinke mee worth thine anger, punish mee,
Burne off my rusts, and my deformity,
Restore thine Image, so much, by thy grace,
That thou may'st know mee, and I'll turne my face.

A Litanie

I: The Father

Father of Heaven, and him, by whom
It, and us for it, and all else, for us
   Thou madest, and govern'st ever, come
And re-create mee, now growne ruinous:
      My heart is by dejection, clay,
      And by selfe-murder, red.
From this red earth, O Father, purge away
All vicious tinctures, that new fashioned
I may rise up from death, before I'am dead.

II: The Sonne

O Sonne of God, who seeing two things,
Sinne, and death crept in, which were never made,
   By bearing one, tryed'st with what stings
The other could thine heritage invade;
      O be thou nail'd unto my heart,
      And crucified againe,
Part not from it, though it from thee would part,
But let it be, by applying so thy paine,
Drown'd in thy blood, and in thy passion slaine.

III: The Holy Ghost

O Holy Ghost, whose temple I
Am, but of mudde walls, and condensed dust,
   And being sacrilegiously
Halfe wasted with youths fires, of pride and lust,
      Must with new stormes be weatherbeat;
      Double in my heart thy flame,
Which let devout sad teares intend; and let
(Though this glasse lanthorne, flesh, do suffer maime)
Fire, Sacrifice, Priest, Altar be the same.

IV: The Trinity

O Blessed glorious Trinity,
Bones to Philosophy, but milke to faith,
  Which, as wise serpents, diversly,
Most slipperinesse, yet most entanglings hath,
      As you distinguish'd undistinct
      By power, love, knowledge bee,
Give mee a such selfe different instinct
Of these; let all mee elemented bee,
Of power, to love, to know, you unnumbered three.

V: The Virgin Mary

For that faire blessed Mother-maid,
Whose flesh redeem'd us; That she-Cherubin,
  Which unlock'd Paradise, and made
One claime for innocence, and disseiz'd sinne,
      Whose wombe was a strange heav'n, for there
      God cloath'd himselfe, and grew,
Our zealous thankes wee poure. As her deeds were
Our helpes, so are her prayers; nor can she sue
In vaine, who hath such titles unto you.

VI: The Angels

And since this life our nonage is,
And wee in Wardship to thine Angels be,
  Native in heavens faire Palaces,
Where we shall be but denizen'd by thee,
      As th'earth conceiving by the Sunne,
      Yeelds faire diversitie,
Yet never knowes which course that light doth run,
So let mee study, that mine actions bee
Worthy their sight, though blinde in how they see.

VII: The Patriarches

And let thy Patriarches Desire
(Those great Grandfathers of thy Church, which saw
  More in the cloud, then wee in fire,
Whom Nature clear'd more, then us Grace and Law,
      And now in Heaven still pray, that wee
      May use our new helpes right,)
Be satisfy'd, and fructifie in mee;
Let not my minde be blinder by more light
Nor Faith, by Reason added, lose her sight.

VIII: The Prophets

Thy Eagle-sighted Prophets too,
Which were thy Churches Organs, and did sound
  That harmony, which made of two
One law, and did unite, but not confound;
      Those heavenly Poëts which did see
      Thy will, and it expresse
In rythmique feet, in common pray for mee,
That I by them excuse not my excesse
In seeking secrets, or Poëtiquenesse.

IX: The Apostles

And thy illustrious Zodiacke
Of twelve Apostles, which ingirt this All,
  (From whom whosoever do not take
Their light, to darke deep pits, throw downe, and fall,)
      As through their prayers, thou'hast let mee know
      That their bookes are divine;
May they pray still, and be heard, that I goe
Th'old broad way in applying; O decline
Mee, when my comment would make thy word mine.

X: *The Martyrs*

And since thou so desirously
Did'st long to die, that long before thou could'st,
   And long since thou no more couldst dye,
Thou in thy scatter'd mystique body wouldst
      In Abel dye, and ever since
      In thine; let their blood come
To begge for us, a discreet patience
Of death, or of worse life: for Oh, to some
Not to be Martyrs, is a martyrdome.

XI: *The Confessors*

Therefore with thee triumpheth there
A Virgin Squadron of white Confessors,
   Whose bloods betroth'd, not marryed were,
Tender'd, not taken by those Ravishers:
      They know, and pray, that wee may know,
      In every Christian
Hourly tempestuous persecutions grow;
Tentations martyr us alive; A man
Is to himselfe a Dioclesian.

XII: *The Virgins*

The cold white snowie Nunnery,
Which, as thy mother, their high Abbesse, sent
   Their bodies backe againe to thee,
As thou hadst lent them, cleane and innocent,
      Though they have not obtain'd of thee,
      That or thy Church, or I,
Should keep, as they, our first integrity;
Divorce thu sinne in us, or bid it die,
And call chast widowhead Virginitie.

XIII: *The Doctors*

Thy sacred Academie above
Of Doctors, whose paines have unclasp'd, and taught
   Both bookes of life to us (for love
To know thy Scriptures tells us, we are wrote
     In thy other booke) pray for us there
     That what they have misdone
Or mis-said, wee to that may not adhere;
Their zeale may be our sinne. Lord let us runne
Meane waies, and call them stars, but not the Sunne.

XIV

And whil'st this universall Quire,
That Church in triumph, this in warfare here,
   Warm'd with one all-partaking fire
Of love, that none be lost, which cost thee deare,
     Prayes ceaslesly,'and thou hearken too,
     (Since to be gratious
Our taske is treble, to pray, beare, and doe)
Heare this prayer Lord: O Lord deliver us
From trusting in those prayers, though powr'd out thus.

XV

From being anxious, or secure,
Dead clods of sadnesse, or light squibs of mirth,
   From thinking, that great courts immure
All, or no happinesse, or that this earth
     Is only for our prison fram'd,
     Or that thou art covetous
To them whom thou lovest, or that they are maim'd
From reaching this worlds sweet, who seek thee thus,
With all their might, Good Lord deliver us.

XVI:

From needing danger, to bee good,
From owing thee yesterdaies teares to day,
From trusting so much to thy blood,
That in that hope, wee wound our soule away,
From bribing thee with Almes, to excuse
Some sinne more burdenous,
From light affecting, in religion, newes,
From thinking us all soule, neglecting thus
Our mutuall duties, Lord deliver us.

XVII

From tempting Satan to tempt us,
By our connivence, or slack companie,
From measuring ill by vitious,
Neglecting to choake sins spawne, Vanitie,
From indiscreet humilitie,
Which might be scandalous,
And cast reproach on Christianitie,
From being spies, or to spies pervious,
From thirst, or scorne of fame, deliver us.

XVIII

Deliver us for thy descent
Into the Virgin, whose wombe was a place
Of middle kind; and thou being sent
To'ungratious us, staid'st at her full of grace;
And through thy poore birth, where first thou
Glorifiedst Povertie,
And yet soone after riches didst allow,
By accepting Kings gifts in the Epiphanie,
Deliver, and make us, to both waies free.

XIX

And through that bitter agonie,
Which is still the agonie of pious wits,
   Disputing what distorted thee,
And interrupted evennesse, with fits;
      And through thy free confession
      Though thereby they were then
Made blind, so that thou might'st from them have gone,
Good Lord deliver us, and teach us when
Wee may not, and we may blinde unjust men.

XX

Through thy submitting all, to blowes
Thy face, thy clothes to spoile; thy fame to scorne,
   All waies, which rage, or Justice knowes,
And by which thou could'st shew, that thou wast born;
      And through thy gallant humblenesse
      Which thou in death did'st shew,
Dying before thy soule they could expresse,
Deliver us from death, by dying so,
To this world, ere this world doe bid us goe.

XXI

When senses, which thy souldiers are,
Wee arme against thee, and they fight for sinne,
   When want, sent but to tame, doth warre
And worke despaire a breach to enter in,
      When plenty, Gods image, and seale
      Makes us Idolatrous,
And love it, not him, whom it should reveale,
When wee are mov'd to seeme religious
Only to vent wit, Lord deliver us.

XXII

In Churches, when th'infirmitie
Of him which speakes, diminishes the Word,
  When Magistrates doe mis-apply
To us, as we judge, lay or ghostly sword,
      When plague, which is thine Angell, raignes,
      Or wars, thy Champions, swaie,
When Heresie, thy second deluge, gaines;
In th'houre of death, the'Eve of last judgement day,
Deliver us from the sinister way.

XXIII

Heare us, O heare us Lord; to thee
A sinner is more musique, when he prayes,
  Then spheares, or Angels praises bee,
In Panegyrique Allelujaes;
      Heare us, for till thou heare us, Lord
      We know not what to say;
Thine eare to'our sighes, teares, thoughts gives voice and
    word.
O Thou who Satan heard'st in Jobs sicke day,
Heare thy selfe now, for thou in us dost pray.

XXIV

That wee may change to evennesse
This intermitting aguish Pietie;
  That snatching cramps of wickednesse
And Apoplexies of fast sin, may die;
      That musique of thy promises,
      Not threats in Thunder may
Awaken us to our just offices;
What in thy booke, thou dost, or creatures say,
That we may heare, Lord heare us, when wee pray.

That our eares sicknesse wee may cure,
And rectifie those Labyrinths aright;
 That wee, by harkning, not procure
Our praise, nor others dispraise so invite;
  That wee get not a slipperinesse
  And senslesly decline,
From hearing bold wits jeast at Kings excesse,
To'admit the like of majestie divine;
That we may locke our eares, Lord open thine.

That living law, the Magistrate,
Which to give us, and make us physicke, doth
 Our vices often aggravate,
That Preachers taxing sinne, before her growth,
  That Satan, and invenom'd men
  Which well, if we starve, dine,
When they doe most accuse us, may see then
Us, to amendment, heare them; thee decline:
That we may open our eares, Lord lock thine.

That learning, thine Ambassador,
From thine allegeance wee never tempt,
 That beauty, paradises flower
For physicke made, from poyson be exempt,
  That wit, borne apt high good to doe,
  By dwelling lazily
On Natures nothing, be not nothing too,
That our affections kill us not, nor dye,
Heare us, weake ecchoes, O thou eare, and cry.

XXVIII

Sonne of God heare us, and since thou
By taking our blood, owest it us againe,
   Gaine to thy self, or us allow;
And let not both us and thy selfe be slaine;
     O Lambe of God, which took'st our sinne
     Which could not stick to thee,
O let it not returne to us againe,
But Patient and Physition being free,
As sinne is nothing, let it no where be.

Upon the translation of the Psalmes by Sir Philip Sydney, *and the Countesse of Pembroke, his Sister*

Eternall God, (for whom who ever dare
Seeke new expressions, doe the Circle square,
And thrust into strait corners of poore wit
Thee, who art cornerlesse and infinite)
I would but blesse thy Name, not name thee now;
(And thy gifts are as infinite as thou:)
Fixe we our prayses therefore on this one,
That, as thy blessed Spirit fell upon
These Psalmes first Author in a cloven tongue;
(For 'twas a double power by which he sung
The highest matter in the noblest forme;)
So thou hast cleft that spirit, to performe
That worke againe, and shed it, here, upon
Two, by their bloods, and by thy Spirit one;
A Brother and a Sister, made by thee
The Organ, where thou art the Harmony.
Two that make one *John Baptists* holy voyce,
And who that Psalme, *Now let the Iles rejoyce,*
Have both translated, and apply'd it too,
Both told us what, and taught us how to doe.
They shew us Ilanders our joy, our King,
They tell us *why*, and teach us *how* to sing;
Make all this All, three Quires, heaven, earth, and sphears;
The first, Heaven, hath a song, but no man heares,
The Spheares have Musick, but they have no tongue,
Their harmony is rather danc'd than sung;
But our third Quire, to which the first gives eare,
(For, Angels learne by what the Church does here)
This Quire hath all. The Organist is hee
Who hath tun'd God and Man, the Organ we:

183

The songs are these, which heavens high holy Muse
Whisper'd to *David*, *David* to the Jewes:
And *Davids* Successors, in holy zeale,
In formes of joy and art doe re-reveale
To us so sweetly and sincerely too,
That I must not rejoyce as I would doe
When I behold that these Psalmes are become
So well attyr'd abroad, so ill at home,
So well in Chambers, in thy Church so ill,
As I can scarce call that reform'd untill
This be reform'd; Would a whole State present
A lesser gift than some one man hath sent?
And shall our Church, unto our Spouse and King
More hoarse, more harsh than any other, sing?
For *that* we pray, we praise thy name for *this*,
Which, by [this] *Moses* and this *Miriam*, is
Already done; and as those Psalmes we call
(Though some have other Authors) *Davids* all:
So though some have, some may some Psalmes translate,
We thy Sydnean Psalmes shall celebrate,
And, till we come th'Extemporall song to sing,
(Learn'd the first hower, that we see the King,
Who hath translated those translators) may
These their sweet learned labours, all the way
Be as our tuning; that, when hence we part,
We may fall in with them, and sing our part.

To Mr Tilman *after he had taken orders*

Thou, whose diviner soule hath caus'd thee now
To put thy hand unto the holy Plough,
Making Lay-scornings of the Ministry,
Not an impediment, but victory;
What bringst thou home with thee? how is thy mind
Affected since the vintage? Dost thou finde
New thoughts and stirrings in thee? and as Steele
Toucht with a Loadstone, dost new motions feele?
Or, as a Ship after much paine and care,
For Iron and Cloth brings home rich Indian ware,
Hast thou thus traffiqu'd, but with farre more gaine
Of noble goods, and with lesse time and paine?
Thou art the same materials, as before,
Onely the stampe is changed; but no more.
And as new crowned Kings alter the face,
But not the monies substance; so hath grace
Chang'd onely Gods old Image by Creation,
To Christs new stampe, at this thy Coronation;
Or, as we paint Angels with wings, because
They beare Gods message, and proclaime his lawes,
Since thou must doe the like, and so must move,
Art thou new feather'd with cœlestiall love?
Deare, tell me where thy purchase lies, and shew
What thy advantage is above, below.
But if thy gainings doe surmount expression,
Why doth the foolish world scorne that profession,
Whose joyes passe speech? Why do they think unfit
That Gentry should joyne families with it?
As if their day were onely to be spent
In dressing, Mistressing and complement;
Alas poore joyes, but poorer men, whose trust
Seemes richly placed in sublimed dust;

(For, such are cloathes and beauty, which though gay,
Are, at the best, but of sublimed clay.)
Let then the world thy calling disrespect,
But goe thou on, and pitty their neglect.
What function is so noble, as to bee
Embassadour to God and destinie?
To open life, to give kingdomes to more
Than Kings give dignities; to keepe heavens doore?
Maries prerogative was to beare Christ, so
'Tis preachers to convey him, for they doe
As Angels out of clouds, from Pulpits speake;
And blesse the poore beneath, the lame, the weake.
If then th'Astronomers, whereas they spie
A new-found Starre, their Opticks magnifie,
How brave are those, who with their Engine, can
Bring man to heaven, and heaven againe to man?
These are thy titles and preheminences,
In whom must meet Gods graces, mens offences,
And so the heavens which beget all things here,
And the earth our mother, which these things doth beare,
Both these in thee, are in thy Calling knit,
And make thee now a blest Hermaphrodite.

A Hymne to Christ, at the Authors last going into Germany

In what torne ship soever I embarke,
That ship shall be my embleme of thy Arke;
What sea soever swallow mee, that flood
Shall be to mee an embleme of thy blood;
Though thou with clouds of anger do disguise
Thy face; yet through that maske I know those eyes,
    Which, though they turne away sometimes,
      They never will despise.

I sacrifice this Iland unto thee,
And all whom I lov'd there, and who lov'd mee;
When I have put our seas twixt them and mee,
Put thou thy sea betwixt my sinnes and thee.
As the trees sap doth seeke the root below
In winter, in my winter now I goe,
    Where none but thee, th'Eternall root
      Of true Love I may know.

Nor thou nor thy religion dost controule,
The amorousnesse of an harmonious Soule,
But thou would'st have that love thy selfe: As thou
Art jealous, Lord, so I am jealous now,
Thou lov'st not, till from loving more, thou free
My soule: Who ever gives, takes libertie:
    O, if thou car'st not whom I love
      Alas, thou lov'st not mee.

Seale then this bill of my Divorce to All,
On whom those fainter beames of love did fall;
Marry those loves, which in youth scattered bee
On Fame, Wit, Hopes (false mistresses) to thee.
Churches are best for Prayer, that have least light:
To see God only, I goe out of sight:
    And to scape stormy dayes, I chuse
      An Everlasting night.

The Lamentations of Jeremy, for the most part according to Tremelius

1 How sits this citie, late most populous,
   Thus solitary, and like a widdow thus!
Amplest of Nations, Queene of Provinces
   She was, who now thus tributary is!

2 Still in the night shee weepes, and her teares fall
   Downe by her cheekes along, and none of all
Her lovers comfort her; Perfidiously
   Her friends have dealt, and now are enemie.

3 Unto great bondage, and afflictions
   Juda is captive led; Those nations
With whom shee dwells, no place of rest afford,
   In streights shee meets her Persecutors sword.

4 Emptie are the gates of Sion, and her waies
   Mourne, because none come to her solemne dayes.
Her Priests doe groane, her maides are comfortlesse,
   And shee's unto her selfe a bitternesse.

5 Her foes are growne her head, and live at Peace,
   Because when her transgressions did increase,
The Lord strooke her with sadnesse: Th'enemie
   Doth drive her children to captivitie.

6 From Sions daughter is all beauty gone,
   Like Harts, which seeke for Pasture, and find none,
Her Princes are, and now before the foe
   Which still pursues them, without strength they go.

7 Now in her daies of Teares, Jerusalem
   (Her men slaine by the foe, none succouring them)
Remembers what of old, shee esteemed most,
   Whilest her foes laugh at her, for what she hath lost.

8 Jerusalem hath sinn'd, therefore is shee
 Remov'd, as women in uncleannesse bee;
Who honor'd, scorne her, for her foulnesse they
 Have seene; her selfe doth groane, and turne away.

9 Her foulnesse in her skirts was seene, yet she
 Remembred not her end; Miraculously
Therefore shee fell, non comforting: Behold
 O Lord my affliction, for the Foe growes bold.

10 Upon all things where her delight hath beene,
 The foe hath stretch'd his hand, for shee hath seene
Heathen, whom thou command'st, should not doe so,
 Into her holy Sanctuary goe.

11 And all her people groane, and seeke for bread;
 And they have given, only to be fed,
All precious things, wherein their pleasure lay:
 How cheape I'am growne, O Lord, behold, and weigh.

12 All this concernes not you, who passe by mee,
 O see, and marke if any sorrow bee
Like to my sorrow, which Jehova hath
 Done to mee in the day of his fierce wrath?

13 That fire, which by himselfe is governed
 He hath cast from heaven on my bones, and spred
A net before my feet, and mee o'rthrowne,
 And made me languish all the day alone.

14 His hand hath of my sinnes framed a yoake
 Which wreath'd, and cast upon my neck, hath broke
My strength. The Lord unto those enemies
 Hath given mee, from whom I cannot rise.

15 He under foot hath troden in my sight
 My strong men; He did company invite

To breake my young men; he the winepresse hath
    Trod upon Juda's daughter in his wrath.

16 For these things doe I weepe, mine eye, mine eye
    Casts water out; For he which should be nigh
To comfort mee, is now departed farre;
    The foe prevailes, forlorne my children are.

17 There's none, though *Sion* do stretch out her hand,
    To comfort her, it is the Lords command
That *Jacobs* foes girt him. *Jerusalem*
    Is as an uncleane woman amongst them.

18 But yet the Lord is just, and righteous still,
    I have rebell'd against his holy will;
O heare all people, and my sorrow see,
    My maides, my young men in captivitie.

19 I called for my *lovers* then, but they
    Deceiv'd mee, and my Priests, and Elders lay
Dead in the citie; for they sought for meat
    Which should refresh their soules, they could not get.

20 Because I am in streights, *Jehova* see
    My heart o'rturn'd, my bowells muddy bee,
Because I have rebell'd so much, as fast
    The sword without, as death within, doth wast.

21 Of all which heare I mourne, none comforts mee,
    My foes have heard my griefe, and glad they be,
That thou hast done it; But thy promis'd day
    Will come, when, as I suffer, so shall they.

22 Let all their wickednesse appeare to thee,
    Doe unto them, as thou hast done to mee,
For all my sinnes: The sighs which I have had
    Are very many, and my heart is sad.

1 How over Sions daughter hath God hung
   His wraths thicke cloud! and from heaven hath flung
To earth the beauty of *Israel*, and hath
   Forgot his foot-stoole in the day of wrath!

2 The Lord unsparingly hath swallowed
   All Jacobs dwellings, and demolished
To ground the strengths of *Juda*, and prophan'd
   The Princes of the Kingdome, and the land.

3 In heat of wrath, the horne of *Israel* hee
   Hath cleane cut off, and lest the enemie
Be hindred, his right hand he doth retire,
   But is towards *Jacob*, All-devouring fire.

4 Like to an enemie he bent his bow,
   His right hand was in posture of a foe,
To kill what *Sions* daughter did desire,
   'Gainst whom his wrath, he poured forth, like fire.

5 For like an enemie *Jehova* is,
   Devouring *Israel*, and his Palaces,
Destroying holds, giving additions
   To *Juda's* daughters lamentations.

6 Like to a garden hedge he hath cast downe
   The place where was his congregation,
And *Sions* feasts and sabbaths are forgot;
   Her King, her Priest, his wrath regardeth not.

7 The Lord forsakes his Altar, and detests
   His Sanctuary, and in the foes hand rests
His Palace, and the walls, in which their cries
   Are heard, as in the true solemnities.

8 The Lord hath cast a line, so to confound
  And levell *Sions* walls unto the ground;
He drawes not back his hand, which doth oreturne
  The wall, and Rampart, which together mourne.

9 Their gates are sunke into the ground, and hee
  Hath broke the barres; their King and Princes bee
Amongst the heathen, without law, nor there
  Unto their Prophets doth the Lord appeare.

10 There *Sions Elders* on the ground are plac'd,
  And silence keepe; Dust on their heads they cast,
In sackcloth have they girt themselves, and low
  The Virgins towards ground, their heads do throw.

11 My bowells are growne muddy, and mine eyes
  Are faint with weeping: and my liver lies
Pour'd out upon the ground, for miserie
  That sucking children in the streets doe die.

12 When they had cryed unto their Mothers, where
  Shall we have bread, and drinke? they fainted there,
And in the streets like wounded persons lay
  Till 'twixt their mothers breasts they went away.

13 *Daughter Jerusalem,* Oh what may bee
  A witnesse, or comparison for thee?
Sion, to ease thee, what shall I name like thee?
  Thy breach is like the sea, what help can bee?

14. For thee vaine foolish things thy Prophets sought,
  Thee, thine iniquities they have not taught,
Which might disturne thy bondage: but for thee
  False burthens, and false causes they would see.

15 The passengers doe clap their hands, and hisse,
  And wag their head at thee, and say, Is this

That citie, which so many men did call
   Joy of the earth, and perfectest of all?

16 Thy foes doe gape upon thee, and they hisse,
   And gnash their teeth, and say, Devoure wee this,
For this is certainly the day which wee
   Expected, and which now we finde, and see.

17 The Lord hath done that which he purposed,
   Fulfill'd his word of old determined;
He hath throwne downe, and not spar'd, and thy foe
   Made glad above thee, and advanc'd him so.

18 But now their hearts against the Lord do call,
   Therefore, O walls of *Sion*, let teares fall
Downe like a river, day and night; take thee
   No rest, but let thine eye incessant be.

19 Arise, cry in the night, poure, for thy sinnes,
   Thy heart, like water, when the watch begins;
Lift up thy hands to God, lest children dye,
   Which, faint for hunger, in the streets doe lye.

20 Behold O Lord, consider unto whom
   Thou hast done this; what, shall the women come
To eate their children of a spanne? shall thy
   Prophet and Priest be slaine in Sanctuary?

21 On ground in streets, the yong and old do lye,
   My virgins and yong men by sword do dye;
Them in the day of thy wrath thou hast slaine,
   Nothing did thee from killing them containe.

22 As to a solemne feast, all whom I fear'd
   Thou call'st about mee; when thy wrath appear'd,
None did remaine or scape, for those which I
   Brought up, did perish by mine enemie.

1 I am the man which have affliction seene,
   Under the rod of Gods wrath having beene,
2 He hath led mee to darknesse, not to light,
   3 And against mee all day, his hand doth fight.

4 Hee hath broke my bones, worne out my flesh and skinne,
   5 Built up against mee; and hath girt mee in
With hemlocke, and with labour; 6 and set mee
   In darke, as they who dead for ever bee.

7 Hee hath hedg'd me lest I scape, and added more
   To my steele fetters, heavier then before.
8 When I crie out, he out shuts my prayer: 9 And hath
   Stop'd with hewn stone my way, and turn'd my path.

10 And like a Lion hid in secrecie,
   Or Beare which lyes in wait, he was to mee.
11 He stops my way, teares me, made desolate,
   12 And hee makes mee the marke he shooteth at.

13 Hee made the children of his quiver passe
   Into my reines, 14 I with my people was
All the day long, a song and mockery.
   15 Hee hath fill'd mee with bitternesse, and he

Hath made me drunke with wormewood. 16 He hath burst
   My teeth with stones, and covered mee with dust;
17 And thus my Soule farre off from peace was set,
   And my prosperity I did forget.

18 My strength, my hope (unto my selfe I said)
   Which from the Lord should come, is perished.
19 But when my mournings I do thinke upon,
   My wormwood, hemlocke, and affliction,

20 My Soule is humbled in remembring this;
  21 My heart considers, therefore, hope there is.
22 'Tis Gods great mercy we'are not utterly
  Consum'd, for his compassions do not die;

23 For every morning they renewed bee,
  For great, O Lord, is thy fidelity.
24 The Lord is, saith my Soule, my portion,
  And therefore in him will I hope alone.

25 The Lord is good to them, who on him relie,
  And to the Soule that seeks him earnestly.
26 It is both good to trust, and to attend
  (The Lords salvation) unto the end:

27 'Tis good for one his yoake in youth to beare;
  28 He sits alone, and doth all speech forbeare,
Because he hath borne it. 29 And his mouth he layes
  Deepe in the dust, yet then in hope he stayes.

30 He gives his cheekes to whosoever will
  Strike him, and so he is reproched still.
31 For, not for ever doth the Lord forsake,
  32 But when he'hath strucke with sadnes, hee doth take

Compassion, as his mercy'is infinite;
  33 Nor is it with his heart, that he doth smite;
34 That underfoot the prisoners stamped bee,
  35 That a mans right the Judge himselfe doth see

To be wrung from him, 36 That he subverted is
  In his just cause; the Lord allowes not this.
37 Who then will say, that ought doth come to passe,
  But that which by the Lord commanded was?

38 Both good and evill from his mouth proceeds;
  39 Why then grieves any man for his misdeeds?
40 Turne wee to God, by trying out our wayes;
  41 To him in heaven, our hands with hearts upraise.

42 Wee have rebell'd, and falne away from thee,
  Thou pardon'st not; 43 Usest no clemencie;
Pursuest us, kill'st us, coverest us with wrath,
  44 Cover'st thy selfe with clouds, that our prayer hath

No power to passe. 45 And thou hast made us fall
  As refuse, and off-scouring to them all.
46 All our foes gape at us. 47 Feare and a snare
  With ruine, and with waste, upon us are.

48 With watry rivers doth mine eye oreflow
  For ruine of my peoples daughter so;
49 Mine eye doth drop downe teares incessantly,
  50 Untill the Lord looke downe from heaven to see.

51 And for my citys daughters sake, mine eye
  Doth breake mine heart. 52 Causles mine enemy,
Like a bird chac'd me. 53 In a dungeon
  They have shut my life, and cast on me a stone.

54 Waters flow'd o'r my head, then thought I, I am
  Destroy'd; 55 I called Lord, upon thy name
Out of the pit. 56 And thou my voice didst heare;
  Oh from my sigh, and crye, stop not thine eare.

57 Then when I call'd upon thee, thou drew'st nere
  Unto mee, and said'st unto mee, do not feare.
58 Thou Lord my Soules cause handled hast, and thou
  Rescud'st my life. 59 O Lord do thou judge now,

Thou heardst my wrong. 60 Their vengeance all they
    have wrought;
  61 How they reproach'd, thou hast heard, and what they
    thought,
62 What their lips uttered, which against me rose,
    And what was ever whisper'd by my foes.

63 I am their song, whether they rise or sit,
    64 Give them rewards Lord, for their working fit,
65 Sorrow of heart, thy curse. 66 And with thy might
    Follow, and from under heaven destroy them quite.

CHAP. IV

1 How is the gold become so dimme? How is
    Purest and finest gold thus chang'd to this?
The stones which were stones of the Sanctuary,
    Scattered in corners of each street do lye.

2 The pretious sonnes of Sion, which should bee
    Valued at purest gold, how do wee see
Low rated now, as earthen Pitchers, stand,
    Which are the worke of a poore Potters hand.

3 Even the Sea-calfes draw their brests, and give
    Sucke to their young; my peoples daughters live,
By reason of the foes great cruelnesse,
    As do the Owles in the vast Wildernesse.

4 And when the sucking child doth strive to draw,
    His tongue for thirst cleaves to his upper jaw.
And when for bread the little children crye,
    There is no man that doth them satisfie.

5 They which before were delicately fed,
    Now in the streets forlorne have perished,
And they which ever were in scarlet cloath'd,
    Sit and embrace the dunghills which they loath'd.

6 The daughters of my people have sinned more,
   Then did the towne of *Sodome* sinne before;
Which being at once destroy'd, there did remaine
   No hands amongst them, to vexe them againe.

7 But heretofore purer her Nazarite
   Was then the snow, and milke was not so white;
As carbuncles did their pure bodies shine,
   And all their polish'dnesse was Saphirine.

8 They are darker now then blacknes, none can know
   Them by the face, as through the streets they goe,
For now their skin doth cleave unto the bone,
   And withered, is like to dry wood growne.

9 Better by sword then famine 'tis to dye;
   And better through pierc'd, then through penury.
10 Women by nature pitifull, have eate
   Their children drest with their owne hands for meat.

11 *Jehova* here fully accomplish'd hath
   His indignation, and powr'd forth his wrath,
Kindled a fire in *Sion*, which hath power
   To eate, and her foundations to devour.

12 Nor would the Kings of the earth, nor all which live
   In the inhabitable world beleeve,
That any adversary, any foe
   Into *Jerusalem* should enter so.

13 For the Priests sins, and Prophets, which have shed
   Blood in the streets, and the just murthered:
14 Which when those men, whom they made blinde, did
   stray
   Thorough the streets, defiled by the way.

With blood, the which impossible it was
Their garments should scape touching, as they passe,
198

15 Would cry aloud, depart defiled men,
  Depart, depart, and touch us not; and then

They fled, and strayd, and with the *Gentiles* were,
  Yet told their friends, they should not long dwell there;
16 For this they are scattered by Jehovahs face
  Who never will regard them more; No grace

Unto their old men shall the foe afford,
  Nor, that they are Priests, redeeme them from the sword.
17 And wee as yet, for all these miseries
  Desiring our vaine helpe, consume our eyes:

And such a nation as cannot save,
  We in desire and speculation have.
18 They hunt our steps, that in the streets wee feare
  To goe: our end is now approached neere,

Our dayes accomplish'd are, this the last day.
  19 Eagles of heaven are not so swift as they
Which follow us, o'r mountaine tops they flye
  At us, and for us in the desart lye.

20 The annointed Lord, breath of our nostrils, hee
  Of whom we said, under his shadow, wee
Shall with more ease under the Heathen dwell,
  Into the pit which these men digged, fell.

21 Rejoyce O *Edoms daughter*, joyfull bee
  Thou which inhabitst *Huz*, for unto thee
This cup shall passe, and thou with drunkennesse
  Shalt fill thy selfe, and shew thy nakednesse.

22 And then thy sinnes O *Sion*, shall be spent,
  The Lord will not leave thee in banishment.
Thy sinnes O *Edoms daughter*, hee will see,
  And for them, pay thee with captivitie.

1 Remember, O Lord, what is fallen on us;
    See, and marke how we are reproached thus,
2 For unto strangers our possession
    Is turn'd, our houses unto Aliens gone,

3 Our mothers are become as widowes, wee
    As Orphans all, and without father be;
4 Waters which are our owne, wee drunke, and pay,
    And upon our owne wood a price they lay.

5 Our persecutors on our necks do sit,
    They make us travaile, and not intermit,
6 We stretch our hands unto th'*Egyptians*
    To get us bread; and to the *Assyrians*.

7 Our Fathers did these sinnes, and are no more,
    But wee do beare the sinnes they did before.
8 They are but servants, which do rule us thus,
    Yet from their hands none would deliver us.

9 With danger of our life our bread wee gat;
    For in the wildernesse, the sword did wait.
10 The tempests of this famine wee liv'd in,
    Black as an Oven colour'd had our skinne:

11 In *Judaes* cities they the maids abus'd
    By force, and so women in *Sion* us'd.
12 The Princes with their hands they hung; no grace
    Nor honour gave they to the Elders face.

13 Unto the mill our yong men carried are,
    And children fell under the wood they bare.
14 Elders, the gates; youth did their songs forbeare,
15   Gone was our joy; our dancings, mournings were.

16 Now is the crowne falne from our head; and woe
    Be unto us, because we'have sinned so.
17 For this our hearts do languish, and for this
    Over our eyes a cloudy dimnesse is.

18 Because mount *Sion* desolate doth lye,
    And foxes there do goe at libertie:
19 But thou O Lord art ever, and thy throne
    From generation, to generation.

20 Why should'st thou forget us eternally?
    Or leave us thus long in this misery?
21 Restore us Lord to thee, that so we may
    Returne, and as of old, renew our day.

22 For oughtest thou, O Lord, despise us thus,
    And to be utterly enrag'd at us?

Hymne to God my God, in my sicknesse

Since I am comming to that Holy roome,
  Where, with thy Quire of Saints for evermore,
I shall be made thy Musique; As I come
  I tune the Instrument here at the dore,
  And what I must doe then, thinke here before.

Whilst my Physitians by their love are growne
  Cosmographers, and I their Mapp, who lie
Flat on this bed, that by them may be showne
  That this is my South-west discoverie
  Per fretum febris, by these streights to die,

I joy, that in these straits, I see my West;
  For, though theire currants yeeld returne to none,
What shall my West hurt me? As West and East
  In all flatt Maps (and I am one) are one,
  So death doth touch the Resurrection.

Is the Pacifique Sea my home? Or are
  The Easterne riches? Is *Jerusalem*?
Anyan, and *Magellan*, and *Gibraltare*,
  All streights, and none but streights, are wayes to them,
  Whether where *Japhet* dwelt, or *Cham*, or *Sem*.

We thinke that *Paradise* and *Calvarie*,
  Christs Crosse, and *Adams* tree, stood in one place;
Looke Lord, and finde both *Adams* met in me;
  As the first *Adams* sweat surrounds my face,
  May the last *Adams* blood my soule embrace.

So, in his purple wrapp'd receive mee Lord,
  By these his thornes give me his other Crowne;
And as to others soules I preach'd thy word,
  Be this my Text, my Sermon to mine owne,
  Therfore that he may raise the Lord throws down.

A Hymne to God the Father

I

Wilt thou forgive that sinne where I begunne,
  Which is my sin, though it were done before?
Wilt thou forgive those sinnes through which I runne,
  And doe them still: though still I do deplore?
    When thou hast done, thou hast not done,
      For, I have more.

II

Wilt thou forgive that sinne by which I wonne
  Others to sinne? and, made my sinne their doore?
Wilt thou forgive that sinne which I did shunne
  A yeare, or two: but wallowed in, a score?
    When thou hast done, thou hast not done,
      For, I have more.

III

I have a sinne of feare, that when I have spunne
  My last thred, I shall perish on the shore;
Sweare by thy selfe, that at my death thy Sunne
  Shall shine as it shines now, and heretofore;
    And, having done that, Thou hast done,
      I have no more.

Index of First Lines

205